Betrayal

BETRAYAL

The Struggle for Cricket's Soul

GRAEME WRIGHT

H. F. & G. WITHERBY

First published in Great Britain 1993
by H. F. & G. Witherby
A Cassell imprint
Villiers House, 41/47 Strand, London WC2N 5JE
Second impression July 1993

A catalogue record for this book
is available from the British Library

ISBN 0 85493 226 7

Photoset in Great Britain by
Rowland Phototypesetting Ltd, Bury St Edmunds, Suffolk
and printed in Great Britain by
Butler & Tanner Ltd, Frome, Somerset

For Karen

Acknowledgements

I am indebted to the following authors and publishers for their kind permission to use passages quoted in the writing of this book: Jack Bailey, *Conflicts in Cricket* (The Kingswood Press); Andrew Hignell, *The History of Glamorgan County Cricket Club* (Christopher Helm); Derek Hodgson, *The Official History of Yorkshire County Cricket Club* (The Crowood Press); Richard Streeton, *P. G. H. Fender: a biography* (Faber and Faber); Collins Willow, *Barclays World of Cricket*, ed. E. W. Swanton; Hodder & Stoughton Ltd, *The Changing Anatomy of Britain* by Anthony Sampson, *Lord's* by Geoffrey Moorhouse and *M.C.C. The Autobiography of a Cricketer* by Colin Cowdrey; Jonathan Cape, *The Pendulum Years: Britain and the Sixties* by Bernard Levin; Methuen London Ltd, *The Players: a social history of the professional cricketer* by Ric Sissons (The Kingswood Press); Lennard Associates, *I Don't Bruise Easily* by Brian Close (Macdonald and Jane's) and *From Larwood to Lillee* by Trevor Bailey and Fred Trueman (Queen Anne Press); Macmillan London Ltd, *The Audit of War: the illusion and reality of Britain as a great nation* by Correlli Barnett; Penguin Books, *Roots* by Arnold Wesker; The Peters Fraser & Dunlop Group Ltd, *Anatomy of Britain* and *Anatomy of Britain Today* by Anthony Sampson (Hodder & Stoughton Ltd); and A. P. Watt Ltd, on behalf of The Trustees of the Robert Graves Copyright Trust, *1805* by Robert Graves. My grateful thanks are also extended to the publishers of *The Cricketer* and *Wisden Cricketers' Almanack*.

All photographs courtesy Patrick Eagar.

Whenever a thing changes and alters its nature,
at that moment comes the death of what it was before.

Lucretius

Contents

I

The Spirit of the Age

In November 1962, at the winter meeting of the Advisory County Cricket Committee at Lord's, the representatives of the first-class counties and the minor counties voted by a majority of eleven to seven to end the distinction between the amateur and the professional in English first-class cricket. In future all players would be called cricketers. Although, thirty years on, this decision seems little more than a semantic adjustment, ending what, in the words of the Cricket Correspondent of *The Times*, had 'at last become an anachronism', it was to effect a wider change in the game than simply the removal of a social status. In time, it would influence how county cricket in England was played, administered and financed.

Yet four years earlier, in the spring of 1958, the Advisory Committee had unanimously approved the report of an MCC Special Committee that had rejected abolishing the distinction between amateurs and professionals. Established to look into the problems of amateur status 'in the light of present-day conditions', and comprising leading players and administrators of the period, this MCC committee believed that 'the distinctive status of the amateur cricketer was not obsolete, was of great value to the game and should be preserved'. Leadership and the general approach to the game traditionally associated with the amateur were emphasized; removing the distinction was not considered to be a possible solution to the problems encountered by the amateur.

If nothing else, the change of heart was in keeping with the spirit of the age. Change was a constant theme of the sixties in

Britain. Hemlines changed, not always for the better, standards changed, often overnight, and leisure activities kept apace with the changes. Dissatisfaction found a voice, indeed many voices, and institutions that had stood unquestioned for most of the century felt the winds of change and tacked accordingly. So it was MCC rather than the counties that raised again the issue of amateur and professional status, its Cricket Inquiry Committee asking the counties to report on any significant change since they had approved the amateur definitions laid down in 1958, and to consider the possibility of defining all first-class players as cricketers. When the counties did find that there was a hardening of opinion against the distinction – particularly amongst administrators – it was the full MCC committee that endorsed the Advisory Committee's recommendation to abolish it. An MCC committee, moreover, that contained six members of the earlier Special Committee, including its chairman, the Duke of Norfolk. In fairness to the Duke, and also to G. O. 'Gubby' Allen, neither was at the meeting on 31 January 1963 that anointed the amateur first-class cricketer with consecrated oil.

'As so often in the Sixties,' Bernard Levin wrote – on something quite different from but not entirely unrelated to cricket – 'a principle which had not been seriously questioned for centuries was abandoned as soon as it *was* questioned . . .'* The editor of *Wisden*, however, was not prepared to abandon the principle of the amateur's place in cricket without voicing a few fears. 'We have inherited the game of cricket . . . In the time of W. G. Grace there was talk that the amateur received liberal expenses. Whether this was true or not, I do not believe cricket, as we know it today, would be such a popular attraction, or so remunerative to the professional, without the contribution which Dr Grace and his contemporaries made as amateurs. By doing away with the amateur, cricket is in danger of losing the spirit of freedom and gaiety which the best amateur players brought to the game.'†

Leaving aside for the time being the constant concern about

* Bernard Levin. *The Pendulum Years: Britain and the Sixties* (Jonathan Cape, 1970)
† *Wisden Cricketers' Almanack 1963*

declining attendances, it is none the less worth recalling that only two years earlier Alec Bedser had written in *Wisden* that the rewards of playing cricket were not 'very great and, with advanced education and higher wages, there are safer and definitely more attractive prospects for the average youngster outside the game'. At the time, as Ric Sissons pointed out in his social history of the professional cricketer,* 'a leading Surrey player [as Bedser had been] – the best paid professional cricketer in England – could expect to earn between £900 and £1000 from the county. From that he would have to deduct his away expenses, maintain and renew his equipment and, of course, pay tax. The average male earnings in the manufacturing sector were about £750 gross.' I remember a leading English cricketer, who played as an amateur, telling me that he had looked to make £1000 from cricket when he went into the game after the Second World War.

The irony was that, while MCC was closing the social gap between the gentleman and the player, and the distinction was losing its significance in other walks of life, Britain could not bring itself to abandon the albatross entirely. Advancing his vision of a 'scientific revolution' to the Labour Party Conference in October 1963, Harold Wilson drew attention to what he considered an anomaly of the age. 'At the very time when even the MCC has abolished the distinction between amateur and professional, we are content to remain, in science and industry, a nation of gentlemen in a world of players.'

Wilson was a player, unashamedly professional in his approach to political life, attacking the 'Edwardian establishment mentality' of the Conservative government when in opposition; once prime minister, operating 'a kind of "government by boredom", in which pretensions and passions dissolved in the dry atmosphere of technical discussion',† he produced a Britain that was bleak and grey, in cycles efficient but only rarely vigorous.

Wilson's 'Edwardian establishment' jibe was aimed at Harold Macmillan, a gentleman whose pursuit of power rivalled a player's

* Ric Sissons. *The Players* (The Kingswood Press, 1988)
† Anthony Sampson. *Anatomy of Britain Today* (Hodder & Stoughton, 1965)

pursuit of fifties and hundreds: Levin, again, saw him more as a strolling player – 'a down-at-heel actor resting between engagements at the decrepit theatres of minor provincial towns.'* But when, in 1963, Macmillan resigned, the Conservatives turned not to a Peter May figure, an amateur with a professional approach, but to a man of true amateur inclination in Sir Alec Douglas-Home. Something of an all-rounder, right fast-medium and a batsman of the upper order, Sir Alec, then Lord Dunglass, opened the batting for Eton against Harrow at Lord's in 1921, Gubby Allen's last year in the XI, and with 66 was top-scorer there the following year. He did not win a Blue at Oxford in what were strong years for Cambridge, but was able to play ten first-class games in all, including two for Middlesex while he was at the university. Transposing his first-class batting and bowling averages would suggest a useful talent. Nevertheless he put his cricket experience to better use than writing of it for cricket magazines and the national newspapers. Visiting his brother William in prison at Wormwood Scrubs during the Second World War – the future playwright had been court-martialled, cashiered and incarcerated for disobeying an order to attack Le Havre, which at the time contained many civilians – the future prime minister could not bring himself to look at his brother because he had grown a beard. Instead he spent his time discussing cricket with a warder. It was, indeed, fortunate for both parties that his lordship had come into the game too late to find himself batting with W. G. Grace. Conversations he may have had with King George V remain a matter for his biographers.

The Fourteenth Earl of Home's renunciation of his peerage, in order to contest a seat in the House of Commons, had been made possible by the determined campaign of Anthony Wedgwood Benn, the sometime Viscount Stansgate, which led to the passing of the Peerage Act in July 1963. It was this principle – automatic elevation to the peerage – that had not been seriously questioned for centuries and yet was abandoned as soon as it was questioned.

Douglas-Home, to apply John Woodcock's description of the amateur/professional divide in cricket, was something of an anach-

---

* Bernard Levin. *The Pendulum Years: Britain and the Sixties*

ronism, albeit, as someone said, an elegant one. But, 'floating on the lethargic sea of his own simplicity',* he was hardly a match for Wilson, lost two general elections in seventeen months, and must have struck members of MCC as an admirable choice when Lt-General Sir Oliver Leese nominated him as president of the club in 1966. Reform may have swept through the Grace Gates on the prevailing wind of change; Titmus, F. J., may at last have become F. J. Titmus. But some things never change. W. F. Deedes' reflection, in 1968, that the decisions emanating from the Long Room at Lord's had not been markedly less distinguished than those that had come from the Cabinet Room at No. 10 seems cause for concern whichever way you look at it.

The abolition of amateur and professional status was not the only change introduced by MCC and the counties in 1963. Almost a century after such a competition was first mooted, a national knockout tournament found its way on to the fixture list that season. To be played in one day, weather permitting, it was sponsored by the razor makers Gillette, who gave a block grant of £6500 to be divided equally among the seventeen first-class counties, a trophy, and Man of the Match awards.

The commercialization of cricket had begun. Over the next three decades, sponsorship, not just of county competitions but of Test matches, the sale of broadcasting rights and the intensive marketing of the game put millions of pounds into English cricket. They also changed the nature of the county game so that it became 'a somewhat distant relation to the "meadow game with the beautiful name" that was played and watched for unsophisticated recreation'.† The gate-paying spectator, as distinct from the county member and the Test-match attender, was already a fast-diminishing species at first-class matches, having found other avenues of entertainment. Now, however, a new, less discerning audience came in large numbers to watch the one-day, limited-overs competitions. The John Player League, offering a biff-bang

---

* Bernard Levin. *The Pendulum Years: Britain and the Sixties*
† J. M. Kilburn in *Barclays World of Cricket*; Ed. E. W. Swanton (Willow Books, 1986)

menu of instant cricket and easy access to ale on Sunday afternoons, proved particularly popular. Another new customer, the
corporate hospitality guest, boosted attendances further, until it
seemed to some that the quality of cricket played had become less
important than the financial return on the way the game was sold.
The badge of the county member, once so vital to the game's
economy, was considered in time secondary to the sponsor's logo.

By the 1990s, profits from one-day internationals and Test
matches were making such an essential contribution to county
clubs' balance sheets that in 1992 a majority of counties voted to
reduce the number of matches played in the County Championship, as well as in one of the one-day competitions, to bring about
– so it was claimed – an improvement in the playing standard of
English cricketers. That more spectators might be drawn to county
cricket if the first-class game were made more entertaining, by
providing vigorous, entertaining cricket, was not on the agenda.
What was considered important was a successful England team
that would be the flagship of cricket's marketing campaign.

In the thirty years since the passing of the amateur, and the
introduction of commercial sponsorship, the struggle for the
economic survival of county cricket has given way to the struggle
for the soul of the game. At the same time, cricket was mirroring
changes in English society, as the expectation of egalitarianism
engendered in Harold Wilson's sixties foundered on the cult of the
personality and gave way in time to the aggressive self-enhancing
materialism of Margaret Thatcher's eighties. In the nineties, as the
spirit of free enterprise was snared in the net of recession, flair
and individuality in cricket came to be seen as a threat to success
and were cast aside in favour of the new conformity based on
team commitment. What had once been described as a team game
played by eleven individuals was becoming little more than a team
game.

Technically, as well as socially, cricket went through many
changes in these decades, both in the way the game was played
and the way in which it was administered. The oligarchic MCC
handed over its power to a supposedly more democratic TCCB,
while on the field cricket took on an increasingly gladiatorial

aspect, 'the violence and ferocity of our age expressing itself in cricket', as C. L. R. James wrote of earlier times. The proliferation of one-day cricket reflected the modern age's apparent appetite for simplicity, an impatience with the long view and, instead, a demand for instant gratification and a disdain for what was subtle. Like Bagehot's scattered headless middle-class, 'well-meaning but aimless, wishing to be wise but ignorant how to be wise', the young men, the tired men took not to 'pure art but to showy art; not that which permanently relieves the eye and makes it happy whenever it looks, and as long as it looks, but *glaring* art which catches and arrests the eye for a moment, but which in the end fatigues it.'*

Among cricket-lovers concern grew that the game was betraying its inheritance in order to further short-term policies, looking no farther ahead than each season's balance-sheet. Sometimes, watching county cricket, I have felt that the players themselves were selling the game short by appearing more like salaried employees than entertainers. 'These days you only get to see players,' Harold Larwood told a recent interviewer. 'They are not cricketers. In our time only cricketers played cricket.' A subtle distinction, perhaps, but no less valid for that.

Cricketers do not have to be clowns or characters to provide entertaining cricket. But if cricket is to be a game in which individual feats and personalities make an impact on the public, those who play it for a paying public must be more than clerks, clock-conscious and average-conscious. Sir Neville Cardus held that 'It is more than a game, this cricket. It somehow holds the mirror up to English nature.' If this pertains today, it should make us question what English nature, and indeed Englishness, is if it is mirrored by the modern game.

---

* Walter Bagehot. *Wordsworth, Tennyson, and Browning; or, Pure, Ornate and Grotesque Art in English Poetry* (Essay in the *National Review*, November 1864)

2

A Question of Attitude

The decision, a radical one for MCC, to abolish the distinction between the amateur and the professional cricketer could hardly have come at a more appropriate time. Britain was on the brink of a great period of illusion: indeed, a period of great illusion. Having ridden into the decade high on the expectation, anticipation even, of entering the Common Market, the country had seen its hopes humiliatingly crushed by de Gaulle's veto and was in danger of thinking it could exist in some kind of contented isolation. Cricket's illusion was that it could sustain a fully professional game as a business at a time when attendances had been on the wane for more than a decade.

Or was it an illusion? All but a few of the first-class cricketers in England were already professionals. In 1959 only thirty-nine amateurs appeared in the County Championship and fewer than half that number played in ten or more fixtures.* The age of the amateur had passed, his salad days belonging to those leisure years made possible by the profits of Victorian technology. Now the prosperous years were fast becoming memories, and the middle classes were having to work when once there had been time for cricket. 'People don't often realize,' Harold Macmillan said, 'that the Victorian Age was only an interruption in British history. The hundred years of British naval and to some extent political supremacy which ended in 1914 was a very rare thing in history

* Ric Sissons. *The Players*

. . . we can't expect it to happen again.'* In the decades to come, as we have found, there would be a new age of leisure, resulting in part from a new technology but not the product of profit. An enforced leisure. There would be few finding time for cricket, and even fewer finding themselves sympathetic with Macmillan's premise that it was 'exciting living on the edge of bankruptcy'.

More than the position of the county amateur, the MCC Special Committee examining amateur status in 1957 and 1958 had been concerned with ensuring that the leading amateur cricketers were not prevented 'by present-day economies' from going abroad on major MCC tours. It also wanted to eliminate any serious anomalies that existed in relation to amateur status, and to safeguard the interests of the professional.

The Committee accepted that most players, if any, could no longer afford to play first-class cricket at their own expense. But, while agreeing that cricketers carrying out full-time administrative duties with their county should be regarded as amateurs, they stressed that anyone who was directly or indirectly paid for playing cricket – by a county or by any associated organization – should be considered a professional. Concern was voiced about the problem of the 'pseudo assistant-secretary' who might be paid for playing 'under the umbrella of his nominal secretarial duties', and about the over-liberal interpretation of the word 'expenses'. In the Committee's opinion, expenses should be restricted to those incurred during a match, 'including meals during travelling and gratuities', with an additional allowance for laundry and the upkeep of equipment. As for amateurs selected for major overseas tours, they should be compensated for loss of earnings by a system of broken-time payments.

In classifying all players as cricketers, however, did MCC really intend that all first-class cricketers should be contracted professionals? In its Spring Annual of 1962, *The Cricketer* magazine had sounded a warning that 'If the amateur is driven off, he will, like John Willes of old, ride away out of cricket forever . . . A change will not bring a single new player in, and it may well

* Anthony Sampson. *Anatomy of Britain* (Hodder & Stoughton, 1962)

divert some out.' No-balled in 1822 for what was later legalized as round-arm bowling, Willes, playing for Kent against MCC, is said to have thrown the ball down 'in disgust' and ridden away out of 'Lord's and out of cricket history'. How lucky, Raymond Robertson-Glasgow later wrote, to have a horse as assistant to so comprehensive a retirement.

It was certainly not MCC's intention to drive the amateur out of cricket history. The MCC secretary's annual address to the county secretaries in December 1964 indicates as much. Making a plea for the non-contracted player, S. C. 'Billy' Griffith reminded his audience that their 'wise and far-thinking decision to eliminate the distinction between amateurs and professionals in county cricket had many objects. One was the encouragement of the casual player; the player who did not rely on cricket for his livelihood, who could play, without financial difficulty, for part of the season. It was hoped that, in this way, your playing staff would be cut down in size. By and large this has not happened, and the county game has, in my view, suffered accordingly.'

What interests me about England is the way its institutions have given the all-rounder rein to express himself. Not the bowler who bats and the batsman who bowls, but the man who can turn his mind and talents with some accomplishment to a variety of enterprises. There is a quintessential Englishness about him. Industry and empire, essentially British, relied initially on a different kind: a non-institutional man of vision, single-minded, dogged and usually mistrusted. In an attempt to get the best of both worlds, the Test and County Cricket Board in 1989 appointed Ted Dexter as chairman of its new England Committee to work alongside the England team manager, Micky Stewart: the embodiment, some thought, of the amateur captain and the senior professional of old. But in the chairman they did not get a true amateur all-rounder so much as a dilettante – a particularly apt description, if not strictly etymologically correct, for the Milan-born Dexter.

In general, however, the part-timer is unbeloved of modern professionals and bureaucrats. The professional regards warily any intrusion into his inner circle. The bureaucrat likes to see square pegs in square holes, and preferably before lunch. The decision of Middlesex County Cricket Club, in 1987, to turn down Phil Edmonds' suggestion that he play for them periodically as an amateur illustrated current thinking. It also deprived a great many spectators, if not all, of the enjoyment of watching an entertaining cricketer, albeit one who usually managed to exasperate those in authority. When in 1992 Edmonds, now forty-one, answered Middlesex's call for his left-arm spin, arriving at Trent Bridge for their County Championship game against Nottinghamshire in a silver Rolls-Royce, he demonstrated during twenty-eight overs (10 maidens, 48 runs, 4 wickets) the price English cricket was paying for its reluctance to accommodate the part-time cricketer. It also reinforced a belief that, in moving away from the amateur towards the professional, English society had been landed with the full-time technician and was the poorer for it.

In contemplating the prospect of a place for the non-contracted player, I would emphasize that I am thinking of the cricketer with a genuine talent: the class player rather than the journeyman. I am not advocating a return to the days when amateurs were pencilled in by captains in April for matches that coincided with the amateurs' annual holidays. This may have given some professionals a much-needed rest, but it must have frustrated others. None the less, there should be an opportunity available for good cricketers who, for career reasons, have chosen not to become professional cricketers, yet who have the ability to make a positive contribution to the game, particularly from the point of view of improving cricket as a spectator sport.

Most people connected with county cricket today would argue that the best players come into the game anyway; that the gulf between the county and the club cricketer is wide. And in support of their argument they can point to the results of games between the counties and the minor counties in the limited-overs competitions, though this is not necessarily a fair field for comparison. 'I am tired of hearing county players refer to club cricket as a different game,' MCC secretary Griffith said in 1967, 'creating a mystique about county cricket which ill becomes it and can do nothing but harm. I would like to see club cricketers given their chance alongside the Cowdreys, the Graveneys, the Titmuses and so on.' It is true that the standard of bowling and fielding is higher in the first-class county game, and so it should be. Players have the chance to work on their skills every day of the week. The club cricketer, if he practises at all, does so in far less demanding circumstances. None the less, with the growth of competitive league cricket throughout England, the standard of club cricket improves all the time.

Before making his one-match comeback for Middlesex, Phil Edmonds spent the previous Saturday afternoon in the indoor school at Lord's, where he forestalled any speculation by the Sunday-paper journalists with asides about invitations to play for various country house teams. That practice, however, was sufficient to prevent the Nottinghamshire batsmen from taking him to the cleaners. While it is true that class will always triumph, it does need the opportunity.

Writing about Edmonds brings to mind his Cambridge contemporary, Bill Snowden, since 1984 the master in charge of cricket at Harrow School. Having distinguished himself in his final year at school in 1971 by scoring 1018 runs, hitting four hundreds and playing for the Public Schools at Lord's, under J. R. T. Barclay's captaincy, Snowden won the first of his four Blues as a freshman in 1972. A century against Warwickshire (104 out of a total of 198), and a half-century in the innings victory over Oxford, marked him as a player of promise. At the end of July he was back at Lord's, scoring 80 and 62 for England Young Cricketers in their victory over the Combined Services – G. A. Gooch was not required to bat in either innings – and he then toured the West Indies with that Young England side. A technically sound opening batsman, he scored 434 runs there for an average of 28.93; Gooch, ten months younger, averaged 26.75 for his 317 runs and in Nevis, or was it St Vincent, turned his hand to ball-by-ball commentary for the local radio station.

Snowden captained Cambridge in 1974; Gooch went on to captain Essex and England, though initially his batting, like Snowden's, suffered from the pressures of captaincy. A Cambridge contemporary thought that Snowden made it hard for himself by thinking too much about the game: his first year, when Majid

Khan captained Cambridge, and his last, when he was without the responsibility of the captaincy, were his best. But his last season at Cambridge also proved to be his last in first-class cricket. Although he had enjoyed his taste of first-class cricket, he was unwilling to gamble his early twenties on seasons of Second Eleven cricket, with only limited prospects of breaking into a Lancashire first team containing three England and two overseas Test batsmen. Majid suggested he try his luck at Glamorgan, but instead he went to teach in Barbados. It was not a decision he has since regretted. In addition to furthering his teaching career, he had six enjoyable years playing in a high standard of club cricket against West Indies and island first-class players; as high a standard as he would have experienced had he played county cricket. On the other hand, had it been possible for him to play county cricket on a part-time basis, Snowden thinks he would have been tempted to stay in England to see how far he could go.

Someone who did play county cricket for a time, and would have been the first to avail himself of the opportunity had the mechanism been there to play on a part-time basis, was Mark Faber of Sussex. A grandson of Harold Macmillan, Faber scored 100 for Eton against Harrow in 1968 – the same number of runs the fourteen-year-old Barclay conceded for his six Harrow wickets – and in 1972 he won a Blue for Oxford. In a less utilitarian age his strokeplay would have been an embellishment at Hove; instead, as his obituary in the 1992 *Wisden* recorded, he dropped out of the Sussex side halfway through 1976, 'disenchanted with the spirit and manner in which the game was being played'. Barclay, who went on to captain Sussex, has no doubt that county cricket would have been the richer for Faber's occasional presence.

It is all a question of attitude. Coming into the county game without having to worry about his average or next season's contract, the part-timer is able to play his cricket as a game instead of approaching it as his livelihood. Of course he has to have talent, but talent can be shackled by pressure, rather as a craftsman's skill can be blunted by the economic dictates of the clock. When, after England's defeat by West Indies in 1988, I wrote that 'There is no reason why, in a country where it is often impossible to have building work done or a motor car serviced properly, its sporting tradesmen should perform any better', it was remarked that this sounded like a cry from the heart. I suppose it was. Neither the house in which I live nor the car I drive fits easily into the utilitarian age. Both require time, and although I have been prepared to pay for this time, the professional attitude has been one of getting the job done as quickly as possible, regardless of whether or not the job is finished satisfactorily. Well, first time round anyway. So, instead of being serviced by the so-called professional, my car is attended by a scientist: a part-timer as far as cars are concerned, although this makes him no less skilled in their maintenance. If anything, the evidence suggests a higher level of competence than from the full-time professional.

He does, however, wonder if it might be less enjoyable if he were doing it for a living. As playing cricket often looks less than fun for many doing it for a living, I wonder if there should not be a place for the cricketer who doesn't have to worry about his average and his contract; whose only concern is his talent and his pride in his performance. Ted Dexter might not have been able to tune twin carbs, fit a clutch or run a cyclotron, but in 1968 he did come back after two seasons out of Championship cricket, hit 203 off Kent's bowlers, and play in two Test matches against Australia. True, Dexter is rightly regarded as one of the greatest of modern batsmen, but is there anything to prove that David Gower, say, could not have batted brilliantly for England after only a handful of county games? Apart from administrative convenience, is there really any reason why such a gifted cricketer has to play through the daily grind of an English county season just so he is eligible to represent his country?

3

Occasional Elegance or Recurring Averages

As if to symbolize the passing of cricket's old order, the deaths occurred in 1963 of Sir Pelham Warner and Sir Jack Hobbs: one the archetypal amateur, thought of affectionately as the 'Grand Old Man' of English cricket; the other the model professional who came to be known as 'The Master'. Warner's life *was* cricket, first as a player and subsequently as a writer and administrator. A member of the MCC committee, he became chairman of selectors, had a new stand at Lord's named after him, and in 1950, in his seventy-seventh year, when it was thought the honour had eluded him, he was nominated by the Duke of Edinburgh to be president of MCC.

His entrée into journalism could not have been more in keeping with the amateur tradition. Touring the West Indies with Lord Hawke's side in 1896–97, Warner was the one Lord Hawke turned to when asked if someone could send accounts of the team's games to *The Sportsman* in London. 'Plummy,' said Lord Hawke, 'you're last from school. Why shouldn't you do it?'

For many years Sir Pelham's father was Attorney-General of Trinidad, and it was there, at The Hall in Port-of-Spain, that the young Warner batted on a marble gallery to the bowling of a young West Indian called Killebree, or Humming Bird. It was very different for the young Jack Hobbs, born in Cambridge, where his father was on the staff at Fenner's and was to become the groundsman and umpire to Jesus College. He learned his cricket playing with the college servants on a gravel pitch, with a stump

for a bat and a tennis ball. And whereas Warner was advised at
Rugby and Oxford by professionals, Hobbs taught himself the art
of batsmanship. On all pitches, and especially bad ones, he was
the finest batsman of his generation, possibly of all time, and
his record of 197 first-class centuries becomes more and more
unassailable as first-class cricket diminishes.

In a career stretching over thirty seasons, Hobbs scored 61,237
runs, again the highest aggregate of any first-class cricketer, and
he would have scored thousands more had it not been in his nature
to give someone else a chance when the going was good. Frank
Woolley called him 'the greatest sportsman England ever had',
and in a moving tribute Herbert Sutcliffe, who shared many
famous opening partnerships with him for England, said that
Hobbs 'was a man of the highest integrity who believed in sportsmanship of the highest sense, fair play and clean living. His life
was full of everything noble and true.'

Warner, growing old, fretted that the presidency of MCC would
pass him by. 'I'm a delicate old dog and will not be here much
longer,' he inclined to say. It probably never occurred to the
modest Hobbs that he would be the first professional cricketer
honoured with a knighthood. However, it was Hobbs, returning
from the 1932–33 Ashes series in Australia, who condemned as
contrary to the spirit of cricket the bodyline tactics practised by
England. He did not speak out earlier, he said – he was covering
the tour for a London newspaper – because he 'did not wish to
embarrass Mr Jardine and the team'. Warner, joint-manager of
the touring team, also opposed this kind of bowling; indeed prior
to the tour he had attacked its use by the Yorkshire fast bowler
Bill Bowes against Hobbs in a game at The Oval. But in Australia
Warner said nothing, his admiration for Jardine as a man and as
a captain overcoming his dislike of his methods, even though they
were harming both the game of cricket and England's reputation
for fair play. '. . . if I had to choose between betraying my country
and betraying my friend,' wrote E. M. Forster, 'I hope I should
have the guts to betray my country.'

In 1963 Hobbs spoke of his sadness at the passing of the amateurs, reflecting that it signalled the end of an era in cricket. 'They

were a great asset to the game, much appreciated by all of us because they were able to come in and play freely, whereas many professionals did not feel they could take any chances. Now times are different, and I can understand the position of the amateur who has to make his living. You cannot expect him to refuse good offers outside cricket.'

Thirty years on, with England in the hands of another former Surrey professional, Micky Stewart, we find one of the few cricketers prepared to take chances not being given a chance by his country. My early influences being Calvin more than Cowdrey, I am not by nature of the Gower persuasion. But the cricket memories that remain from impressionable years are of players hitting the ball with majesty: Tom Graveney leaning into a drive which sent the ball between cover and extra-cover with an unhurried grace; John Reid, New Zealand's captain, down on one knee and sweeping the ball flat for six into the picket fence, square leg never moving and the ball not describing the merest hint of a parabola.

Cricket, Raymond Robertson-Glasgow claimed, is a human game, and the importance of the Gowers and Graveneys is that, in addition to their ability to please aesthetically and entertain generally, they make cricket communicable. They bring the onlooker into the game, rather than keeping him outside the ring. They also, and this is no less important, uphold what Lord Denning once said was essential to England: that each man should be free to develop his own personality to the full.

More than a century ago Lord Harris wrote in the new weekly, *Cricket*, that nothing is so essential for the production of a good cricketer as that he should see good cricket. Gower's critics would argue that a flat-footed slash presenting a chance to slip, or a wafted hook down the throat of a set-back square leg, is not good cricket. On the other hand, being caught by the wicket-keeper or slips is a fate common to many adventurous left-handers: the majority of deliveries are slanted across them and so the ball leaves them as they play their strokes. The alternative for the left-hander is to develop a better acquaintance with his off stump and cut out shots at balls passing close to or wide of it. As methods go it is pragmatic and parsimonious. Watching Garry Sobers, Graeme

Pollock or David Gower driving through (or in Pollock's case, over) the cover field brings greater satisfaction. John Edrich, concentrating on his off stump and playing straight in the latter half of his career, could not be blamed if occasionally he thought back on his innings of 310 not out against New Zealand in 1965. With five sixes and fifty-two fours, his innings contained more boundaries than Sobers hit when he made his record 365 not out against Pakistan in 1957–58. More recently, by way of comparison, Gooch's 333 against India at Lord's in 1990 contained three sixes and forty-three fours. In that Test against New Zealand at Leeds, Edrich cut and drove ferociously; in later years, playing straighter and scoring mostly on the leg side, he became an accumulator rather than a strokemaker.

Still, we have come to live in an age when, not just in cricket, the flamboyant is discouraged in favour of the utilitarian. Sir Learie, later Lord, Constantine, whose own exciting cricket always favoured the flamboyant, could have been defending David Gower when he wrote in the 1965 *Wisden* that 'Genius has been ruthlessly reprimanded, because "a century one day and a duck the next is not what we need in this country" . . . Genius is slightly mad, and most erratic, but this is not what is wanted. What is wanted is averages . . . Elegance or style would be acceptable, but it must fit into the averages.' Even so, Gower could point to an average of 44.25 for England, in addition to his elegance and style, and still he had to stand aside for more utilitarian players. Graveney suffered a similar fate. It must have something to do with the greyness of the English climate.

Graveney and Edrich finished their careers with more than 100 hundreds. It is doubtful if Gower will. But when his critics observe this, as undoubtedly they will in time, he can remind them of what Lord Constantine told his audience in a speech to the Royal Commonwealth Society. 'I never wanted to make a hundred. Who wants to make a hundred anyway? When I first went in, my immediate object was to hit the ball to each of the four corners of the field. After that, I tried not to be repetitive.'

Hardly surprising, with an attitude like that, that Constantine averaged no more than 24.05 with the bat in his career; and just under twenty in Tests. Not that Constantine bothered about such things, as we have seen. If patriotism is the last refuge of a scoundrel, averages are often the first refuge of the unimaginative. I suppose they mean something, but they don't always say a lot. Take, for instance, the series between England and West Indies in 1963. England scored more runs per 100 balls than did their opponents (43 to 42), and also had the better over-rate. But it was the West Indians who took the plaudits for their entertaining cricket.

In the West Indies in 1959–60, England scored approximately 43 runs per 100 balls, which compares more than favourably with Australia's rate of around 40 in that memorable 1960–61 series against West Indies in Australia. Yet England's determination to insure against defeat in the Caribbean did not provide interesting cricket for the enthusiastic West Indian spectators; nor for their manager, it seems. When he became chairman of selectors in 1962, R. W. V. Robins promised to encourage a more enterprising approach, saying he would not mind losing all five Tests in Australia if England played the right way. Brave words, but they were unfulfilled. England won one Test and lost one in Australia in 1962–63 and 'Overall much of the cricket was grim,' recorded *Wisden*. The series ended with the Sydney crowd booing and slow-handclapping the players off the field; one correspondent to a Sydney newspaper wrote, 'Harvey and Davidson are quitting the game, but they shouldn't be lonely as they are retiring at the same time as 100,000 spectators.' After presiding over an Ashes defeat in England in 1964, Robins and his chosen captain, Dexter, relinquished their respective positions, with the latter turning his attention to that year's general election. His particular interest, as a Conservative Party candidate, was James Callaghan's Cardiff South-East constituency, where he helped to increase the Labour majority by 900 per cent from 868 to 7814. 'My people felt so sorry for him that they stopped heckling him,' Dexter's opponent remembered.

Against Australia in 1964 England called on twenty players; not one of them was Tom Graveney, who that summer became the fifteenth batsman to make 100 hundreds in first-class cricket.

He had to wait until 1966, and his thirty-ninth birthday, for his Test recall, marking it with a glorious innings of 96 against a West Indian attack comprising Hall, Griffith, Sobers and Gibbs. Lauding Graveney's achievement in reaching his milestone in 1964, Neville Cardus bemoaned the age in which cricket had 'tended to change from a sport and artistic spectacle to a competitive materialistic encounter'; in which it was 'natural enough that we have lived to see and extol an honest artisan such as Boycott building his brick wall of an innings'.* Poor Boycott: writing of him from South Africa in 1965 for *The Cricketer*, John Woodcock said, 'He is threatening to become a bore, by reducing even the strokes he has. The half-volley he is treating like a good-length ball.'

The elimination of risk, which was Boycott's purpose, filled Sir Learie Constantine with a foreboding for cricket's future as a sport that could provide pleasure for participants and spectators alike. He recognized in this negative approach the logical progression of a cautious policy whose aim was to insure against defeat; a policy of caution. Integral to it was control of the scoring-rate, principally by the batsmen's occupation of the crease 'for not less than a minimum period of time calculated on the basis that such occupation closes the door to defeat'. It was an attempt to make cricket, for so long regarded as an art, into one of the exact sciences.

Concurrent with this new philosophy of batting were changes in bowling and fielding. Opposed by batsmen who made virtually no attempt to score off anything but bad balls, bowlers were able to maintain a diet of accurate, short-of-a-length, in-slanting deliveries. In doing so they were encouraged not only by the batsmen's defensiveness but also by an lbw law which looked sympathetically at the delivery pitching on the off side of the stumps and swinging or seaming into them. Out of all this emerged a game of cricket in which the batsman's character was manifested in a series of pushes and prods. Reaction, instead of action, became the keyword, and as often as not the result was stalemate. Little wonder that John Edrich was saying in 1970 that three-day

* *Wisden Cricketers' Almanack 1965*

County Championship matches could be won only on bad pitches. Little wonder, too, that the County Championship had ceased to attract any but the most devoted onlookers. There was nothing of worth to look upon.

'I do not really think it is necessary to remind the older players what the game stands for,' Constantine wrote in the 1965 *Wisden*, 'but the youngster who is coached and fed by the present-day method may never truly discover the depth of feeling of joy and ecstasy and often disappointments that cricket alone can create.' Ian Peebles told a story about a Frank Woolley innings at Canterbury that illustrates just how that feeling of joy could be created and shared. The match was between Kent and the 1930 Australians, and Woolley had begun the home team's second innings 'by lathering that very high-class new-ball bowler, Alan Fairfax, against the off-side palings with such gusto and frequency that, after a couple of overs, Alan went to the acting captain, Vic Richardson, in search of advice. "Do you think it's all right bowling at his off stump like this?" "All right?" said Richardson, shocked at the inadequacy of the term. "It's bloody marvellous. We're all enjoying it." '*

Discovery and learning are the same for spectators as for players. The game of push and prod by batsmen, of containment by bowlers instead of attack, is 'not favourable to the due appreciation of pure art – of that art which must be known before it is admired – which must have fastened irrevocably on the brain before you appreciate it – which you must love ere it will seem worthy of your love.'†

There was a time when cricketers, by their deeds, instilled an appreciation and a love of the game in those who played it at a lesser level and watched it at any level. People went to watch a certain player, not because he played for their county but because they knew he would entertain them. The excitement of a day at Lord's would be dashed by Denis Compton's dismissal – though I know of two ladies who saw the funny side of his first-ball

* *The Cricketer*, 19 May 1967
† Walter Bagehot essay: see page 17

dismissal one Saturday and had the temerity to laugh. The stony faces turned in their direction assured them that this was no laughing matter. In their defence, they had been told by their husbands that a Compton innings was unlike anything they would ever see.

When the players lost the will to entertain (or did they feel it was no longer necessary to entertain?) the administrators took to tampering with the Laws and playing conditions in an attempt to make the game more interesting for the public. Little good it did, except to confuse players and public alike. But then that is the way of committees, once described as a noun of quantity signifying many and not signifying much. Billy Griffith put his finger on their worth when he asked the county secretaries in 1964 if it was 'not unreasonable to suggest that committees insist upon their captains carrying out their wishes in the broadest sense without destroying the personality and character which any captain might have to offer. Surely, too, it is vital to county cricket in particular that a captain is understanding, enthusiastic and thoroughly appreciative of the responsibility he carries.' But Griffith realized this was all rhetorical, as his next sentence revealed. 'It sometimes seems to me that committees are fearful of taking a strong line in this request, and this is surely a pity.'

As the years have shown, it was more than a pity. It was a tragedy. Shorn of spectators, because its spectator appeal was limited, cricket turned in time to sponsorship for survival and, appropriately enough in a materialistic age, while the body lived on the spirit passed away. A new cynicism prevailed, as instanced by Somerset's declaration after one over of their innings in a Benson and Hedges Cup tie. At the time there was nothing in the competition's playing regulations to prevent a team declaring: after all, who, when drawing up the regulations, would have anticipated a team sacrificing all known cricketing principles by losing a game? But they had reckoned without the mathematicians and the strategists in the Somerset dressing-room. An almost instant declaration, they had calculated, would prevent second-placed Worcestershire from improving their striking-rate and would guarantee Somerset a place in the quarter-finals, even though they would lose the game. It profited them not. The Test and County Cricket Board disqualified them from the competition for their 'indefensible' action. Still, one has to admit that Somerset could hardly have timed their declaration better. It was 1979, and a new age acclaiming success as the indicator of worth was on the cusp.

4

Whipping in the Soft Centre

Bureaucracy comes more naturally to governments than democracy, and the government of cricket has shown itself to be no exception to this. County club members, electors of committees to represent their interests and those of the club, are only too aware of how the years of creeping centralization have settled cricket's affairs solidly at the London court of the Test and County Cricket Board. We could, of course, play semantics and argue that the TCCB is no more than the counties in central committee; and that the counties are no more than their membership. But that is bunkum, and every county member who, say, opposed the introduction of coloured clothing for the Sunday League – the majority in a survey conducted by the TCCB itself – knows it is bunkum.

In fact, members have known it to be so from the earliest days of sponsored competition, when the Advisory Committee voted to charge them admission to Gillette Cup matches. As is always the way in such things, a good case was made for the charges, but it was a case rooted in expediency of the contrived kind. At a few cup games in 1964, or was it only at one, the visiting team's supporters arrived to find that the gates had been shut earlier in the morning behind the home county's members. Nor was their disappointment or their anger eased by the egress and ingress of those same members throughout the day. What created this anomaly, it was claimed, was the practice whereby home members had free access to their county ground. So the Advisory Committee voted to remove the anomaly. With foresight, it must be argued, there need not have been any problem, for admission could have been guaranteed for the visitors by the sale of advance tickets – though in fairness to those concerned, foresight has never been the strongest point of administrators in most fields, let alone the cricket field.

But the anomaly was not the real problem. The position would have been the same had a large crowd come for a County Championship match; except that it never did any more. No, the real problem was that many of those going to these exciting and very popular new cup games, being members of the home county, were not paying a farthing – other than the membership subscription that they had paid so that they could watch their county's home games. Holy Cowdrey, some low being on high must have thought, look at the money we're losing. So the counties, the majority of them anyway, agreed that everyone must pay admission for Gillette Cup matches. Of course it was stated that money was not the reason for the new regulation, but Nottinghamshire gave the game away when they told an enquiring member that the new charge was 'a rule of the competition, there is nothing we can do about it, and it brings in extra money'.

At other counties, too, members were taking a dim view of this outrageous decision. In the early days of the Gillette Cup, some rounds were played on a Saturday; consequently members were now being surtaxed for a day's 'paid-up' cricket on the one day many of them could attend their county ground. Sadly, no one appears to have challenged this arbitrary decision in court, for depriving members of their right of entry to their own club premises could have been illegal. A recalcitrant MCC member might have taken action, but not being affected by the new charge – MCC did not play in the competition – MCC members continued to come and go at Lord's as if they owned the place, which of course they did.

At Hove, the Sussex members were informed by their committee that the Advisory Committee would transfer their home games to their opponents' ground if the new admission charges were not sanctioned at the Annual General Meeting – assuming that their opponents had agreed to the new charges, I suppose. And the club's president, the Duke of Norfolk, told them he 'thought it would be tragic if Sussex, winners of the [Gillette] cup in its first two seasons, were to grumble and grouse and turn the motion down'.* Well whipped in, the members capitulated. And if they didn't lose their heads they certainly lost all vestige and every illusion of sovereignty they might once have harboured. De Tocqueville's dictum that 'Municipal institutions are to liberty what primary schools are to learning; they put it within reach of the people' was becoming less and less relevant in Britain. Like the local councils in their dealings with Whitehall, the county cricket clubs would discover that, unable to finance themselves fully, they had become impotent against the committees at Lord's.

There was a time when members were accepted as being the foundation on which a county's existence depended. Only a few years before the introduction of the Gillette Cup charge, the secretary of MCC had been telling the county secretaries just how essential their members were. 'It is my belief,' he said, 'that continued success, and in some cases survival, lies in providing members and their families with amenities, facilities and a focal point for social activities not only for the summer months but all the year round. It seems a pity, and uneconomical, that these splendid grounds and buildings are in some cases scarcely used during the seven winter months.' That can still be said today of his own club, which although a members' club, as well as a cricket club, offers next to nothing out of season for MCC members.

By the 1990s, however, the county member had seen his role in his county's affairs diminishing. Changes in accounting methods make direct comparisons difficult, but a glance at figures from one county club's accounts helps to illustrate the point. In 1961, Lancashire's full membership, other subscriptions and gate receipts were twenty per cent greater than salaries, wages and match expenses. Thirty years on, they covered only a third of a similar expenditure. They remained essential – in 1991 they were the second-highest item of income after the TCCB's distribution from central funds – but now they made up only seventeen per cent of the total income. Sponsorship, ground advertising and

---

* Letter to *The Cricketer*, 4 June 1965

catering also made important contributions to a total income in excess of two million pounds and were vigorously pursued. Spiritually a club is its members, the members are the club, but in balance-sheet terms in a bottom-line society, members have become simply another asset; as often as not, in some committeemen's eyes, an irritating one at that.

Lancashire's committee found them so in 1988, when it wanted to raise subscriptions beyond the maximum increase allowed by the club's rules. Needing a two-thirds majority for approval, the committee found itself rebuffed on a show of hands after lively discussion among those attending the Annual General Meeting. One life member called attention to the declining level of facilities offered to members, saying that at Test matches

> Members were like refugees, and at Liverpool he had to hop from one leg to the other in order to see the cricket. At Lytham half the ground was given over to sponsors and at Old Trafford 12,000 members were crammed into the pavilion. However, he said, members would willingly put up with these inconveniences if the county had a team. The club had not won the Championship since before the war and although the players had gone to town in the last month of the season it had been a very disappointing season. Having been a member for over 50 years he had been told the same old story and after the first two matches he realised the team were in the same doldrums they were in every year. Most of the members never saw the club but if the team was playing well then they would come to support. Finally the point was made that the member concerned did not support the increases in subscriptions.*

He could also have pointed out that there was a time when he enjoyed admission to Test matches, free of charge, as part of his membership subscription. That benefit had been taken away from him in 1980 by the TCCB, which had decided that members should pay admission to Test matches and one-day internationals, albeit

---

* Minutes of Lancashire CCC Annual General Meeting, 1988

at a reduced rate. The honorary treasurer's plea that subscriptions were falling annually as a percentage of total income, as the club relied more and more on sponsorship, not surprisingly received short shrift. After all, membership had an upper limit, whereas the club was actively pursuing income from outside sources, and this was bound to increase if it was successful in its pursuits.

But if some members can be refractory, downright rebellious even, there are rarely enough of them. 'In a confrontation with the politics of power,' Lord Hailsham said, 'the soft centre has always melted away': almost always in the mouths of officers and committeemen who have sweet-talked, cajoled and finally threatened it into compliance. While one game is played in front of the pavilion, as often as not another is being acted out behind the closed door marked 'Committee'.

Not even that inner sanctum has been sacrosanct from the manoeuvrings of the TCCB machine, however. The whip hand is invariably the one that holds the purse-strings, and that hand has slipped easily into a pocket at Lord's; not in the Pavilion, but behind the squash courts, where the Test and County Cricket Board rents rooms from its progenitor, the Marylebone Cricket Club.

It is worth wondering whether the counties didn't have more autonomy in the days when MCC was the cricketing authority. Coming together several times a year under the guise of the Advisory County Cricket Committee, the counties were free to cover, partially cover or uncover again the pitches used in Championship games; they could limit or unlimit the number of overs bowled in the first innings of a Championship game; they could bemuse all and sundry with bonus points and first-innings points. They could even extort tolls from their members at Gillette Cup games, and by and large MCC let them get on with it. It may not always have been the best for cricket, but the county chiefs could leave Lord's feeling they had done something. MCC, meanwhile, looked after Test matches and tours, distributed the proceeds among the counties, universities and minor counties, and looked after cricket generally in a benevolent way. Despite its despotic tag it attempted to dictate the best path for cricket to follow, and if this was frequently a circular one, that was often no bad thing. MCC made mistakes, but all in all it administered cricket for the overall good of the beautiful and beloved game.

The conflict between cricket as an ideal and cricket as an industry is not new. The struggle was there in the campaign waged in the 1860s when those of the new amateur faith tried to break the influence of the professionals. A century later we find it in a different guise. While Mr Griffith was telling the county secretaries that county cricket remained the basis of the game in Britain – 'the example to the lower levels; and the general performance of our Test teams . . . a direct reflection of its health' – Doug Insole, chairman of selectors and a member of the MCC committee, was introducing a different emphasis. 'People's opinion of any game reflects what goes on at the top. What they think about it at any given time is conditioned by the results achieved by the national side, and by the way it plays.'

Insole's was the pragmatic view; one seen through the eyes of a businessman. For all that he played as an amateur, captaining Cambridge in 1949 and Essex throughout the fifties, when he played nine times for England, his approach as an administrator was thoroughly professional. Moreover, his influence was immense, culminating in his chairmanship of the Test and County Cricket Board from 1975 to 1978. During this period Test cricket was sponsored for the first time, by Cornhill Insurance, and, while enriching the game, such sponsorship gave the England team an importance that would increase with every passing series.

It was inevitable that this would affect county cricket, and just as inevitable that the losers would be the county members. Inevitable because the standard of county cricket was not good enough to produce the consistently successful England teams necessary to project an image that could be marketed. Inevitable, too, because Britain was on the road from regional diversity to a centralized corporateness that encouraged standardization.

By the early 1960s it was apparent to the more discerning eye that county cricket contained fewer cricketers of Test class than there were during the 1950s. It may not have helped English sensitivity that some of their critics were not English, but the observation was no less valid for that. Nor was it only the England team that was the poorer because of the declining standards. Members, paying to support their counties, deserved better than having to watch mediocre cricketers, particularly when it didn't always look as if those cricketers were even enjoying themselves. Players were forever being encouraged to take a chance and to enjoy their cricket, but so often the pleading fell on deaf ears.

Not even established Test cricketers were immune from inflicting tedium. Against New Zealand at Birmingham in 1965, Ken Barrington took seven and a quarter hours to score 137 runs; at one point, with 85 to his name, he went for twenty overs without scoring. Once into three figures he showed how forcefully he was capable of batting by hitting 14 runs off one over from the off-spinner, Vic Pollard. Whether for his pains or theirs, Insole and his fellow-selectors decided that the public deserved better and they omitted Barrington from the team for the next Test. The message more or less got through. In the Third Test Barrington used just fifteen scoring strokes to reach 53, but overall his 163 claimed five and a half hours. In this time he and John Edrich, his Surrey colleague, added 369 runs and so missed by 13 runs England's highest partnership for the second wicket against all countries. It was also only 42 runs short of England's record for any wicket, the 411 by May and Cowdrey against West Indies in 1957.

Two years later Barrington was scratching his seven-hour itch again, batting six hours and fifty minutes for 109 not out against Pakistan at Trent Bridge before Close called it a day. England's ten-wicket win, after almost two days were lost to bad weather, was used to vindicate Barrington's safety-first approach, but among those who condemned the innings was Sir Learie Constantine. His was a dissenting, if out-voted, voice on the panel that awarded Barrington the Horlicks England batting prize of £100. Another critic, John Woodcock, wrote that too many soporific innings like Barrington's would soon put the sponsors out of business. A Surrey player of the 1950s told me once that it wasn't surprising that attendances at The Oval went into a decline in the 1960s if spectators had to watch 'that Barrington batting'.

Barrington, it has to be added, did score hundreds in all three Tests against Pakistan in 1967 – a formidable achievement against any side – and his average of 58.67 in Test cricket is bettered by only two other Englishmen, Herbert Sutcliffe and Eddie Paynter. Nor was he the only offender when it came to slow scoring. At Lord's that same summer, Middlesex and Hampshire contrived to get through three days of a Championship game without finishing the first innings. *Wisden* records that 'The match received deserved and universal condemnation'. Yet play began brightly enough on the Saturday, with Roy Marshall scoring 153 out of 210 in a little under three and a half hours. After that, though, Hampshire lost their way, 'their laboured batting on a perfect pitch showing a lack of awareness of their mastery', and they meandered into Sunday before declaring at 421 for seven. Middlesex, having lost their first two wickets for 29, adopted equally cautious methods, and those spectators who had ventured to St John's Wood for the first-ever Sunday of county cricket at Lord's must have wondered why they weren't somewhere else. Mercifully the game had to end on Monday evening, by which time Middlesex had reached 371 for seven and Titmus, their captain, was probably satisfied with denying Hampshire two points for a first-innings win – such things being available in those days.

The Middlesex secretary found some suitable gobbledegook to defend his team's tactics, and poor Mr Griffith, at his desk in the Pavilion, must have wondered why he bothered addressing the county secretaries each year. 'Cricket as a game was . . . always meant to be played in a positive way,' he had told them the previous December, recalling an occasion in 1966, 'on a seaside ground, on a good pitch, on a fine Saturday in July, with a good holiday crowd there, the side batting first managed some 140 runs for the loss of four or five wickets by tea time. Cricket utterly without a point, and nothing as far as I know was said except by the Sunday newspapers. Again, a captain on another occasion made it abundantly clear in front of a good crowd that he disapproved of the 65-over limitation [on the first innings in twelve of each county's Championship games in 1966] – and the cricket played as a result of this irresponsible fourth-form behaviour made a complete travesty of the game.' Such performances on a cricket field, he added, should never be allowed to happen.

Yet they continued to happen. In 1984 the counties agreed not to levy fines for slow over-rates – introduced in 1978 to quicken the tempo of Championship matches – in return for a minimum of 117 overs bowled in an uninterrupted day's play. This averaged out at eighteen overs an hour, and it was reported that the county captains were in favour of the change. As the players themselves had had to dig into their own pockets for half the over-rate fines, which incidentally had been imposed for over-rates under nineteen an hour, this was hardly surprising. But could they manage to bowl 117 overs a day? No way! The 117-overs minimum brought slower over-rates and longer days, in some cases stretched until eight o'clock and later, and after one season the daily minimum was reduced to 112 overs, with the system of fines reintroduced for an average rate of fewer than 18.5 overs an hour. A victory for the players, who would be paid more for less, it was a defeat for common sense and for the members, who found themselves paying more for less.

It was all very well for the players and umpires to complain about the long days. Both had had it in their powers to make the days shorter. Instead, what they achieved was a productivity deal any shop steward would have been proud of. The 1984 champions, Essex, captained by one of the circuit's most astute captains, Keith Fletcher, averaged only 15.53 overs an hour that season, which under the fines system subsequently introduced for 1985 would justly have cost them £14,000 of their £15,000 prize money. It may be that the International Cricket Council knew a thing or two, if not much more, when it devised a system of fines for international cricket on the eve, so to speak, of Fletcher's appointment as England team manager in 1992.

Is it that the game is no longer greater than the prize? That concentration on the prize has demeaned the game? During a Test match, as we watched international cricketers pour a pint into a quart-pot, a county captain of the 1980s opined that players no longer showed respect for the game. By way of example, he mentioned how 'joke bowling' was used not only by captains to bring about predestinated declarations but also by batsmen to boost their averages. On the last morning of a three-day match good players, with the ability to attack, would block out the regular bowlers so that the fielding captain was eventually forced to bring on his occasional bowlers to facilitate a declaration. Then the batsmen would feed; oh how they would feed, the twenty-third psalm upon their lips as yet another meaningless six was fished from the waters of comfort.

Or was that movement of the mouth one saw no more than the mastication of Wrigley's spearmint gum?

It is a far cry from the exhortation of Lord Harris, in his letter to *The Times* in February 1931. 'You do well to love it [cricket], for it is more free from anything sordid, anything dishonourable, than any game in the world. To play it keenly, honourably, generously, self-sacrificingly, is a moral lesson in itself, and the classroom is God's air and sunshine. Foster it, my brothers, so that it may attract all who can find time to play it; protect it from anything that would sully it, so that it may be in favour with all men.'

As attendances showed in the 1960s, at a time of proliferating leisure activities, cricket no longer found favour with every man, or woman. 'For poets to be second-rate is a privilege which neither men, nor gods, nor bookstalls ever allowed.' But the poet Horace had not lived in the age of the seven-hour century; men and bookstalls did allow poets to be second-rate, and the gods were no longer called upon except in times of incense and incantations. Cricket, like the car industry, accommodated the second-rate also.

Micky Stewart, when he was captain of Surrey, said that there were too many mediocre cricketers in county cricket, and that these were bad for the public to watch. He was concerned, too, about the number of good players who left the game early, and for this, and the fact that there were some who chose not to go into first-class cricket, he pointed to the financial insecurity of cricket in comparison with the greater rewards available outside the game.[*]

Some twenty years later, when Stewart was appointed England team manager, sponsorship and increased revenue from television

[*] *The Cricketer*, 3 June 1966

and international matches were providing greater security, even if the rewards were not over-generous except for an elite group. The problem of mediocrity, however, had not been eliminated: there were still too many easy runs for batsmen and easy wickets for bowlers. County cricket, now complicated by several varying forms of the game, had long ceased to be a reliable examination of the prospective Test cricketer, with the result that the difference between county cricket and Test cricket was not so much a gap to be minded as a chasm to be bridged. Building that bridge being more than a one-man job, the Test and County Cricket Board gave it to a committee.

In this instance, the noun of quantity signified not many but few; four, in fact: the chairman, Ted Dexter, the England team manager, Micky Stewart, the chief executive of the TCCB, Alan Smith, and the chairman of the TCCB Cricket Committee, Ossie Wheatley, who acted as the Board's representative. The committee was, in effect, a powerbase for Dexter and Stewart, for in addition to replacing the Selection Committee, which had previously chosen England teams, it was given wide-ranging responsibility for the present and future structure of English cricket. It would emerge in time that the Cricket Committee chairman had been empowered by the Board with a right of veto in England Committee decisions, but in no way did this lessen its influence.

All four who initially comprised that committee had captained their counties in the sterile sixties, and with the exception of Wheatley they had played for England then. Significantly, I believe, all four had come into first-class cricket in the fifties when England's Test-match stock, under the selectorial chairmanship of Gubby Allen and the captaincy of Peter May, was high. May was one of the few genuine amateurs playing first-class cricket, but his approach to the game was professional, and he trod comfortably the path put down by Sir Leonard Hutton, the first professional cricketer to captain England. May did not, for example, believe in part-time first-class cricketers: 'It is all or nothing if a player is going to do himself justice.'* As captain of the MCC team in the

---

* *The Cricketer*, Spring 1968

West Indies in 1959–60 he was at odds with Walter Robins, the manager, over the touring team's purpose. Robins thought they were there primarily to entertain; May knew they were there to win, and like his mentors, Hutton and Stuart Surridge, the successful Surrey captain, he had the steel to ensure that the captain, not the manager, was in charge. As the London *Evening News* and its cricket writer, E. M. Wellings, found to their cost, when May successfully sued for libel in 1963, he was also prepared to defend himself against untrue accusations. An article by Wellings had suggested that May broke promises to Surrey, concerning the number of games he would play for them in 1962, and that he was more of a liability than an asset to his county.

Micky Stewart succeeded May as captain of Surrey in 1963. He had played at Lord's in the same Public Schools side as May's younger brother, John, in 1950 – the season when Wellings rated Stewart second to Colin Cowdrey as the Public Schools batsman of the year – and after National Service he made his way to The Oval to begin the life of a professional cricketer. His timing could not have been better, for Surrey had embarked on the winning run that brought them seven successive Championship titles between 1952 and 1958. When Surrey next won the Championship, in 1971, Stewart was captain and able to enjoy the heady wine of success after leading them through the long years of transition. By necessity as much as by nature, his was not a dynamic captaincy, and Alan Gibson probably got it right when he said that Stewart gave 'few favours and expected few. Despite his football associations, there has never been much of the Corinthian about him.' While playing amateur football for Corinthian-Casuals, Stewart had represented England at inside-forward and, had he not been a professional sportsman in Olympic eyes, might have gone to the 1956 Olympic Games. As a professional footballer he played for Charlton Athletic.

The story goes that Stewart's father, a suburban bookmaker, taught him to tear up money, the lesson being that there is more to life than lucre. It was a philosophy that was manifest in his batting early in his career, and it contrasted starkly with that of his team-mate, Barrington. If not exactly lavish with his strokeplay, Stewart could be generous none the less. Barrington, son of a private soldier and denied the privileges of a public school education, always knew he would have to graft for the security that a regular England place would bring. Entertaining strokeplay was a luxury he could not afford.

Time and responsibility curbed Stewart's youthful indulgences, and when in 1963 he opened the innings in four Tests against the fury of Hall and Griffith, with a best score of 87, he won an approving 'He's got guts' from West Indies' captain, Frank Worrell. However, recurring illness on the MCC tour of India that winter cost him his England place, and his Test career was over after eight caps. Talk in 1963 that he might one day captain his country was certainly premature, and probably owed much to a cricketing variation on the Ontological Argument.

By 1970 his tactics as Surrey's captain were being described as unenterprising. 'Stewart has failed to get the best out of his gifted players,' *Wisden* said, and it questioned the ethics of his 'declaration at a low total with nine wickets down, which deprived Kent of a bonus point at the crisis of the Championship'. At the beginning of the 1971 season Sobers, who was captaining Nottinghamshire, rated him an ultra-defensive captain, and in the first week of August he announced that he was giving up the captaincy of Surrey. 'Lately,' he told the press, 'pressures and frustrations have built up so much that I'm not enjoying the game anywhere near the way I did. I'm snapping at my wife and children and I'm sleeping no more than four hours a night. This has got to stop. I now find I'm playing every ball, bowling every ball and fielding every ball. I think the captaincy has cost me over 600 runs a year.' In the event Surrey asked him to reconsider his decision, and the side began the run of five straight victories that swept them towards the Championship title.

Even so, this was a far remove from the Micky Stewart who once tore up money. A new ethos, a 1960s' rationalism, had replaced that abandon; Stewart had become a planner. He would discover, as have prime ministers before and since, that events often run counter to plans, but he did not forsake his plans at the first rebuff, or even at the second and third. He stuck to his dogged course, aware of the lesson he had learned in 1971: just as events run counter to plans, they also in time run parallel to them. He never attempted to gloss over the problems confronting first-class cricket in England, whether it was the state of pitches, the quality of first-class players, or the amount of cricket played by county cricketers. These were sixties concerns and he carried them into the nineties, determined to correct them. With regard to the amount of cricket played, he had had an influential ally in the 1960s in Billy Griffith, who felt that 'very serious consideration must be given to the amount of cricket we ask our cricketers to play . . . I cannot believe that we should countenance a system which requires the player to perform seven days a week . . .'*

As far back as 1966 Stewart was coming down on the side of those who argued for four-day Championship matches – 'I'm sure you would see more attacking cricket on both sides with the maximum of spin bowling,' he wrote in *The Cricketer*† – but he doubted at the time if the pitches were good enough. Particularly interesting, in view of the way the structure of county cricket changed during his years on the England Committee, was his conclusion to that article. 'Cricket is based on tradition, and I personally am a lover of tradition, but if the game suffers because of tradition then tradition must go.'

At the end of 1992 a tradition did go: the three-day Championship game. Since 1988 a limited number of Championship games had been played over four days at either end of the season, but until 1992 the counties had resisted the advances of the England Committee for sixteen four-day games per county, becoming seventeen with the elevation of Durham to first-class status in 1992. What the counties could not resist was the 'all or nothing' package put in front of them by the Middlesex chairman, M. P. Murray, and the working party he set up in 1991 to report on the domestic first-class game. Seventeen four-day matches were the

---

* Address to county secretaries, December 1964
† 3 June 1966

castor oil; a revamped Sunday League, with the prospect of a new sponsor, coloured clothing and television coverage, was the sweetener. The counties swallowed it and their members felt sick.

5

More Than a Game

Working parties, like commissions and enquiries set up by governments, have become so installed in the public consciousness as a
means of preventing change, rather than achieving it, that the
acceptance of his Structure Working Party's report was something
of a triumph for Mr Murray, chairman of the TCCB's Finance
Committee in addition to his county chairmanship. Even after
careful lobbying of the counties by the Board's executive, emphasizing that the proposals had to be accepted in total or else rejected,
it was a close-run thing. The voting was only eleven to eight in
favour, which, given the need for all the counties to pull together,
was not a decisive one.

Still, the majority was sufficient for county members in their
deck chairs, dipping into *The Wealth of Nations* between social
chat, scones and a seam bowler's heavy tread to a distant point,
to nod sagely over Adam Smith's observation that 'The interest
of dealers . . . in any particular branch of trade or manufactures,
is always in some respects different from, and even opposite to,
that of the public.' Members' interests so rarely coincided with
those of the Test and County Cricket Board, it seemed, that they
must at times have wondered if their own representatives on the
Board had not been dipping into Edmund Burke* between gins
and tonics in the committee room.

---

* 'Your representative owes you not his industry only, but his judgement; and he
betrays instead of serving you if he sacrifices it to your opinion.' Edmund Burke, to
the electors of Bristol, 1774

They must have snorted, too, at statistics put forward in defence
of replacing the long-established three-day County Championship
cricket with the four-day game. They were losing no more than
four days of Championship play, they were told; trading 72 days
in 1992 for 68 in 1993. But that was an administrative analysis.
Like most statistics plucked out by self-justifying politicians, these
too failed to relate to the human factor. Few members can attend
every day's play throughout the season, but many could go to one
day of every game. Whereas in 1992 such members could go to
twenty-two Championship games by following their county, now
there were only seventeen. Put even less favourably, from the
members' point of view, they were losing three home games every
alternate season. Added to which was the more dubious depri-
vation incurred by the curtailment of the Benson and Hedges Cup.
Played since its introduction in 1972 in a league/knockout format,
the B & H became a straight knockout competition in 1993. The
one gain was the extension of the Sunday League, relaunched as
the One-day Championship, from forty to fifty overs per side. In
addition, the Sunday games would be 'sandwiched' during the
County Championship, so the dedicated Lancashire supporter
could now watch Yorkshire for five days on the trot – though
probably not at a gallop.

There is, however, another way of looking at this. The majority
of county members, it is fair to say, are not frequent attenders, and
there are those who may not go to games at all, their membership
subscription in itself being their way of supporting their county
and its team. A good turnout can be guaranteed on high days,
and occasionally on holidays, but in the main the newcomer to
County Championship cricket is likely to be surprised by how few
spectators are there. I know I was, just as I was when I first
attended a debate in the House of Commons. As with cricket,
nothing in the newspapers had prepared me for the presence of
only a handful of members. It was almost as if there was a conspiracy to keep the public from knowing that two of the country's
institutions generally enacted their daily routines for the smallest
of minorities.

How greatly this mattered is another question. Parliament and county cricket clubs may be no more than the sum of their members, but government and the game go on with or without their presence. So leaving aside government and concentrating on cricket, perhaps it is worth asking for whom the county game is intended, given that it is so erratically attended. The answer has to be that it is for more than the members. So closely is cricket tied to the life of this country, in a way it is not in other cricket-playing countries, that it must be for every British man and woman. As Tom Brown said at his last school match, 'It's more than a game. It's an institution!' Thomas Hughes, writing his novel in the nineteenth century, might just have been using 'institution' in a recent colloquial form, meaning well established or familiar, but it is more likely he had in mind the sixteenth-century definition which enabled him to place cricket within the social life of the nation's people.

Institutions, though, are worth no more than the men who work them, according to another nineteenth-century writer, the Swiss philosopher Henri Amiel. Names here are not important, for the emphasis is not on the personalities who administer English cricket. Rather it is how their roles within the institution of cricket are perceived, because the roles and the perceptions have altered in the last ten to twenty years. Take, for example, the county secretary, whom the secretary of MCC used to address annually. His position has certainly evolved. In the formative days of the county clubs, it was an honorary one, undertaken usually by someone from the emerging professional or business classes. By the middle of this century, the secretary was a paid official of the club, perceived by some members as a servant of the club. Today, more often than not, the appellation is no longer secretary but chief executive or general manager, titles more in keeping with a business than a club. Which, of course, is how many of cricket's administrators view the game, and is how cricket is run, with marketing managers, commercial managers, catering managers and occasionally, in some clubs, cricket managers.

In 1992 Sussex, advertising for a director of marketing, didn't even think it essential for the applicant to have an interest in cricket, acknowledging only that it would be helpful. It makes you wonder if the club, in considering an interest in cricket non-essential, was acknowledging also that its new director would be marketing not cricket but a product – something for which his 'considerable experience in the world of Marketing' had prepared him. But if cricket is just that, a product to be promoted as part of a business, it has ceased to be more than a game in the sense Tom Brown meant. Cricket has become no more than a car, a beer or a washing-up liquid when it can be marketed by someone who needs no interest in the game, its history and traditions, the emotions it arouses and its place in national life. If that is so, it has not only ceased to be more than a game. More seriously, it has ceased to be an institution.

Disraeli said that a country lives by its institutions, but what Walter Bagehot wrote concerns me more. 'The characteristic danger of great nations, like the Roman, or the English, which have a long history of continuous creation, is that they may at last fail from not comprehending the great institutions they have created.'* Cricket may not be one of *the* great institutions, but it is a great one none the less, and Britain will have lost something when first-class cricket in England and Wales is no more than just a game; no more than a means of making money for marketing men bent on making their mark.

Even now cricket's profile has become registered in an international context rather than a domestic one. Just as British industry has had to come to terms with operating in a competitive international marketplace, so England in cricket has had to adjust to the reality of other countries growing stronger through regular international competition. Not simply improving in playing strength, either, but seeing international cricket as their major source of funding. International success in Test matches and one-day internationals has attracted sponsorship, which in turn has helped countries to keep their best cricketers in the game at the highest level. New Zealand, for so long the Cinderella of Test cricket, illustrates the point well, but so, from a different perspective, does Australia. There was a time when English journalists,

---

* Walter Bagehot. *Essay on Lord Althorp*

frustrated by the tired performances of ageing England Test cricketers, would call for an injection of youth, pointing by way of
example to the success Australia enjoyed through the introduction
of youngsters to Test cricket. It happens less today. Where once
players bowed out of Test cricket while still in their prime, in
order to advance their career prospects, today's Australian Test
cricketer hangs on to his baggy green cap for as long as he is good
enough. His security depends less on what he does outside the
game because it is underwritten by the income that the Australian
Board generates from sponsorship, television and other off-the-
field areas. What happens if Australian television's eye is caught
by a more comely wench does not bear thinking about.

Essential to all the Test-playing countries except England in
recent years has been the development of the squad system, which
brings their leading players together to hone their skills. This has
its disadvantages, but the advantages outweigh them, allowing
the 'weaker' countries to ride more comfortably the troughs of
transition when star players retire. Apart from pre-tour preparation, such a system has not been possible in England because
the players are tied by contract to their counties, for all that the
country they represent is scarcely more than their employers in
corporate clothing. In fact, on a warm day, without his sweater,
the England player looks as if he is representing the Test and
County Cricket Board and a Yorkshire brewery, not England.

The impracticality of having a settled squad system, combined
with the disparity that exists between county cricket and Test
cricket, has placed England at a disadvantage in home series.
(Their greatest home advantage, that of uncovered pitches, has
long been conceded.) This is why the counties were forced to
look beyond their own interests and well beyond their members'
interests, to the extent that we find cricket's democracy looking
remarkably like parliamentary democracy. Rousseau probably got
it right when he wrote that

> The English people believes itself to be free; it is gravely mis-
> taken; it is free only during election of members of parliament;
> as soon as the members are elected, the people are enslaved; it

is nothing. In the brief moment of its freedom, the English people makes such a use of that freedom that it deserves to lose it.

Time, perhaps, to elevate Burke from a footnote to provide a counter-argument: '. . . parliament is a *deliberative* assembly of *one* nation, with *one* interest, that of the whole; where, not local purposes, not local prejudices ought to guide, but the general good, resulting from the general reason of the whole.' Yet where cricket is concerned, there is something of a dichotomy when it comes to the general good and the general reason of the whole. Though connected, they have not necessarily been complementary. Taking cricket's place in national life, we could argue that the general good is England's success in Test cricket, because from that success percolates a general feeling of well-being within the country. This was vividly apparent in 1981 after Botham's heroics at Headingley had opened the way for Willis to charge through Australia. People smiled in the streets – sometimes, even, to one another – and they walked with a lighter step. It wasn't just that England had beaten Australia; it was that the tide had turned and England, their England, was victorious again.

I was first aware of this reaction to cricketing success in March 1968, when England beat West Indies by seven wickets at Port-of-Spain; I could sense as well as see what cricket meant in English life. As far as I could remember, there had been nothing as demonstrative in Wellington, where I was a schoolboy, when New Zealand won a Test for the first time after twenty-six years of trying. There were jubilant scenes at Eden Park, Auckland, where the victory came, but I do not recall the country's psyche being uplifted. In those days only the All Blacks did that.

There was something in the way England won that Test match in Trinidad that made it special. The imagination was fired by England's taking up Sobers' challenge and winning in style. West Indies had dominated the first two days, declaring on the third at 526 for seven, and when England's reply went into the fourth day, victory for the home side or a draw seemed the only possible results. By lunch on the final day, the odds were on a draw. As Colin Cowdrey, England's captain, recalled: 'The whole atmosphere, as we returned to the field after lunch, was one of sleepy indifference. It did not seem then that West Indies were going to declare. The match was dead, we were weary and quite relieved to play the day through.'*

What Cowdrey was unaware of was the discussion that had taken place during the interval between Sobers, the West Indies captain, and Everton Weekes, their manager. They had not yet condemned the match to a draw, but in weighing up their chances of winning they had to balance several factors. On the one hand, the pitch would not favour the spinners to the extent it had in England's first innings. On the other hand, England were known to be diffident against leg-break bowling. In the first innings Basil Butcher, an occasional leg-spinner, had picked up five England wickets for just 15 runs in a spell of ten overs, and in the Trinidadian, Willie Rodriguez, Sobers possessed a leg-break and googly practitioner with match-winning potential on his home ground. It was why he had been brought into the side for this Test. Earlier in the tour, in the island match, Rodriguez had taken six for 51 against MCC.

Sobers' biggest gamble, though, was setting England a target while knowing that his fast bowler, Charlie Griffith, injured in the first innings, would not be available to close the game down if the England batsmen decided to go for the runs. Not that Sobers thought they would. Throughout the game the heat had been intense, and his declaration, asking England to score 215 runs in 165 minutes, was influenced by his belief that the weary Englishmen, suddenly faced with having to bat the match out, could be vulnerable.

In the England dressing-room, however, a much more positive attitude prevailed than the West Indies captain imagined. England reckoned that a good start would give them every chance of achieving their target, and Edrich and Boycott provided this with 55 runs in nineteen overs. After tea Boycott and Cowdrey, adding 100 in eighteen overs, reduced the target to 42 runs in thirty-five

* Colin Cowdrey. M.C.C. *The Autobiography of a Cricketer* (Hodder & Stoughton, 1976)

minutes, and when Cowdrey was out for 71, made in seventy-six minutes of commanding strokeplay, Boycott stayed on to steer England to victory with three minutes to spare. Throughout the Caribbean Sobers was blamed mercilessly for the defeat, but in London West Indians rejoiced with fellow-Britons over a victory well won.

These overseas victories are doubly welcome in that they relieve the gloom of dull winter days or hurry spring along with a promise of summer. At home, though, summer can be clouded by poor England performances, and these are harder to put right. On tour, strong leadership and a good team spirit can set the ship back on course, but in England, where the players disperse as soon as each Test is over, the captain and the team manager have only a day or two before each Test to raise morale. Techniques, too, often need attention, and it can be argued that this would not be necessary with a higher standard of county cricket.

Thus the general good does not in itself result from the general reason of the whole, which I take to be England's summer-long circuit of professional county cricket. Rather, the general reason of the whole has come to be dependent on the general good, which is why the majority of county representatives became, returning again to Burke, 'not member of Bristol, but . . . a member of *parliament*'. In other words they saw their duty lying not with the county members who elected them but with the Test and County Cricket Board and *A Blueprint for the First-Class Game*, as the Structure Working Party's report was titled.

A worrying aspect of the power with which the TCCB has invested itself is the Board's evolution into a commercial enterprise. To all intents and purposes it has become a corporation in miniature, with its executive and its various departments. Indeed, as each pursues its own interests, it can seem as if these departments, like their counterparts in larger corporations, are scarcely part of the same team. The different proposals in 1991 for the Sunday League are just one example of what, if not a struggle for power, is an opportunity for playing at office politics. The TCCB's Cricket Committee, looking to reduce the amount of cricket and travelling required of county cricketers, advocated restructuring the Sunday League in two divisions of eight teams each, with play-offs to determine the season's champions.

From a cricketing point of view this made good sense; indeed it had been a recommendation of the Palmer Report, which in 1986 presented the findings of an enquiry into the standards of play in English Test and county cricket. The League, with its forty-overs format, was technically more damaging to players' techniques, particularly bowlers', than the longer limited-overs competitions. Moreover, a Sunday League played in two divisions, or conferences, had a natural focus for the media and the public with its build-up to the play-offs. Mindful that Sunday cricket was popular with the public, the Cricket Committee also proposed playing Benson and Hedges Cup or County Championship games when there were no Sunday League fixtures.

These proposals found support from only four counties. Instead, the vote went in favour of the existing all-season single-division Sunday League, with the counties playing in coloured clothing and using a white ball against a black sightscreen – Australia's floodlit costume drama down-graded to a daylight nightmare. What would happen when the white ball emerged from the white seating installed at certain English grounds was a matter of juicy conjecture among the staider patrons of county cricket. The pyjama programme was very much the preference of the marketing men, who after all had to sell the League to a sponsor and to television, and they were not averse to the occasional classical retort

*Diversos diversa iuvant, non omnibus annis omnia conveniunt**

against charges of philistinism. Given the commitment to coloured clothing, though, it was surprising that the counties didn't pick up the potential of a two-conference competition. Perhaps they didn't want to be seen to be imitating American baseball, which operates in gaudy gear along conference lines. Imitating Australians was more acceptable.

What had these committees set out to achieve? The Cricket Committee could argue that it was trying to raise the standard of

---

* Various things delight various men; all things are not for all ages.

county cricket in order to improve the prospects of the England team. The Marketing Committee could point to the need to bring in revenue to keep the county game on the road – which was where the county players complained of spending too much time. And yet, while their proposals differed, they were linked in a common purpose, which was intentionally or unintentionally the control by the Board over its constituent counties through the income generated by national sponsorships and the sale of Test match and one-day international tickets.

Having in the England team such an ideal marketing tool, it is only natural that the TCCB should consider its 'principal function and power [to be] the promotion, financing and betterment of cricket generally with an essential object being the achievement of the highest possible standards at international level'.* But the Test match has become a precarious commodity on the international market, where investors have shown a determined, if alarming, preference for the one-day game. England need be wary. There is a limit to the extent to which they can depend even on nationalistic support if the cricket they play is consistently lacking *joie de vivre*.

Much depends on how the players rise to the challenge presented by four-day cricket. The opportunity is there for them to take the initiative in Championship games and to achieve victory through positive batting and attacking and thoughtful bowling, instead of waiting for an agreeable declaration on the final day. But if Russell's Law (Resistance to new ideas increases as the square of their importance) joins forces with Parkinson's Law (Work expands to meet the time available for its completion), nothing will have been achieved and Mr Murray's report will not be worth the word-processing, let alone its glossy four-colour cover. 'He who has his thoughts upon taking, never thinks of what he has taken.'† It would be ironic indeed if, by maintaining their workaday attitude to county cricket and taking it into Test cricket, the players themselves undermined the foundations that the Test and County Cricket Board have put in place to underpin their careers.

---

* The Constitution of the Test and County Cricket Board
† *The Essays of Michel de Montaigne*

6

A Precarious Balance

With the exception of the Sunday League, extended by an hour and twenty minutes' playing time, the Structure Working Party's report of 1992 had much to commend it to the players. It specified a more rational programme, with less travelling and even less cricket, and, by concentrating on the structure of the county game, it did not fall into the trap of tampering with the Laws and the playing conditions. In addition to being a *Blueprint for the First-Class Game*, the report offered a blueprint for a settled county game for a period of at least five years.

It was a different strategy from that adopted in the 1960s. Then, faced with unenterprising cricket and declining attendances, the authorities seemingly had little option but to fumble for a formula that might make the game more attractive to spectators. Despite the success of the new Gillette Cup, there was even an overall reduction in county membership halfway through the decade, raising a genuine concern for the first-class future of some counties. Indeed, in a survey carried out for the enquiry that produced the Clark Report in 1966, many county cricketers voiced fears for their livelihood, giving these as a reason for the negative way they were playing. Twenty-five years on, it should be said, much of the cricket on offer was just as tedious, yet the game was providing a less precarious living.

The success of Frank Worrell's West Indian side in England in 1963 offered one answer to the problem: play enterprising cricket and the public would come to watch it. The authorities saw the answer lying down another road – and their reasoning was just

as clear. After the Australian tour, the traditional drawcard, in
1961, the Board of Control's distribution of profits put
£146,822 in the counties' coffers, while in 1962, when Pakistan
toured, the profit was just over £80,000. The West Indies tour
produced a windfall of £148,356 for distribution. The obvious
answer was to get the West Indians back as soon as possible; the
snag was that they were not due to tour again until 1971. This
realization must have struck Lord's with a devastation similar to
that experienced by the Australian authorities in February 1961
when, with 90,800 people packing the Melbourne Cricket Ground
on the second day of the final Test, it occurred to someone that
nothing had been agreed for West Indies' next tour of Australia.
As it turned out, the Australians had to wait another eight years;
England waited only three for the Caribbean cash register to ring
again.

The West Indians, on course for a healthy share of the Test
takings in 1963, opened the way for a speedy return to England
by suggesting at that year's ICC meeting the possibility of more
frequent visits to England by all overseas countries. With Australia's tours always scheduled on a regular rota, the only way
this could be arranged was if two countries toured in the same
summer. And by good fortune MCC was asked to look into the
feasibility of twin tours, particularly in relation to the financial
ramifications for visiting sides.

This decision may have been unanimous when the ICC delegates
met at Lord's. It was another story when it came to getting agreement from the actual cricketing authorities, with India and Pakistan in particular, and not surprisingly, having objections to the
proposals. India were down for a full tour of England in 1967,
Pakistan in 1969. Under the new schedules, MCC was proposing
that these two countries, hardly the happiest of neighbours, should
share the summer of 1967 and forsake their full tours until a time
to be determined. Not that the alternative – either India or Pakistan sharing a tour with South Africa – presented fewer difficulties.
In the circumstances it must have been a happy coincidence that
MCC, having no major tour arranged for the winter of 1963–64,
was able to send a side to India in January and February to play

five Test matches in eight weeks. 'Financially the tour was a rous-
ing success' – despite the passage of only two years since Dexter's
MCC side played a five-Test series there – 'though the nature of
the play inflicted sore wounds on the game of cricket,' E. M.
Wellings reported in *Wisden*.

Also away from home that January were G. O. 'Gunboat' Allen,
the president of MCC, and the club's secretary, Billy Griffith,
shuttling between India and Pakistan to resolve the differences
over the twin tours. To say a long-distance call from Bombay to
Karachi got Mr Allen nowhere is not strictly true, for it got him
and Mr Griffith on a flight to Karachi, where he learned that the
president of the Pakistan Board of Control was in fact some 900
miles farther north in Rawalpindi. Off they set again, and their
travels were rewarded by a warm welcome, a dinner attended by
'numerous members' of the Pakistan cabinet, and the Pakistanis'
agreement to the twin-tour proposal. Back in Bombay they were
similarly successful with their negotiations, their diplomacy
fortunately not being jeopardized by the MCC team's decision
'to take tinned food from England for use in the more remote
cricketing centres, where European cooking is not understood'.*
Apparently some 'touchy folk' in India were taking mild exception to this.

Buoyed by the bounty brought in by the 1966 West Indian tour,
by the appeal of the one-day competition to a wider audience, and
by the prospect of an Australian tour in 1968, the counties in
1967 threw out the more radical proposals of the Clark Report.
The suggestion that there should be two separate championships,
one with a programme of sixteen three-day matches and the other
of sixteen one-day matches, as well as the Gillette Cup, won the
support of only four counties. (Twenty-five years later, with four-
day matches instead of three, this was the plank with which the
Murray committee beat the counties.) Much more appealing was
Hampshire's proposal that each county be allowed two overseas
players, with their qualifying period reduced from two years to
one, and this romped home by fifteen to five. Nottinghamshire

* *Wisden Cricketers' Almanack 1965*

and Somerset's suggestion that one of the overseas players should be allowed in without any qualification period was rejected. But some time during the rainy summer of 1967 the counties had second thoughts, and that autumn they gave it their assent by a clear two-thirds majority. The editor of *Wisden* had every reason to ask where the money was coming from 'to pay these expensive stars with county cricket in its present parlous state.'*

Although this opened the floodgates for the stream of overseas players who came into county cricket, the wheels had been turning in that direction since early in the decade. The catalyst was the success Australian cricket had enjoyed by employing Garry Sobers, Rohan Kanhai and Wes Hall as guest players for South Australia, Western Australia and Queensland respectively in the 1961–62 Sheffield Shield. Attendances at Shield games that summer demonstrated that fans were prepared to go to see the best cricketers, particularly when opportunities to do so were limited. To attract star players to England, however, several barriers had to be removed. A major one was the regulation that threatened every overseas cricketer's county qualification if he played first-class cricket in or for the country of his birth outside the English season. Between the wars this had cost the Australians the services of several Test cricketers, in particular their great fast bowler, Ted McDonald; Roy Marshall's decision to qualify for Hampshire ended his chances of adding to the four caps he won for West Indies in Australia and New Zealand in 1951–52.

This restriction was lifted in 1962, and at the same time the qualification period for overseas players was reduced from three years to two, bringing it into line with that required of English-born cricketers. At the time, the counties drew the line at an overseas player appearing for his own country on a tour of England, arguing that his county, being his regular employer, would be deprived of the services of one of their outstanding players. Bad enough having to release players for England Test duty! Still, Time plays the fiddle, and it wasn't long before the counties were shuffling their feet to another tune. In 1965 they agreed that overseas

* *Wisden Cricketers' Almanack 1968*

players could join a tour of the United Kingdom by their native country without losing their county qualification.

The injection of overseas players into county cricket was just what the game needed, giving it a vitality which in turn brought in paying customers as well as membership subscriptions. Appropriately the prize catch went to one of the proponents of the instant registration, Nottinghamshire, whose signing of Sobers lifted them from fifteenth in the County Championship in 1967 to fourth in 1968. Glamorgan, strengthened by the acquisition of the gifted Pakistani batsman, Majid Khan, made a similarly impressive rise, jumping eleven places from fourteenth to third, and they might have finished higher had Sobers and Nottinghamshire not demolished their prospects when they visited Swansea at the end of August.

It could have been a game like any other: a year earlier and it probably would have been. But when Garry Sobers sauntered to the wicket, with 308 runs on the board and five wickets down, history was in the making. Before the afternoon was out he would have hit a record six sixes in one over. 'It wasn't sheer slogging through strength,' said Tony Lewis, the Glamorgan captain, afterwards, 'but scientific hitting with every movement working in harmony.' The unfortunate bowler was twenty-three-year-old Malcolm Nash, a left-arm medium-pacer who had chosen the wrong moment in time to experiment with left-arm spin.

The first two balls disappeared high over the heads of the mid-wicket fielders and into the crowd sitting in the stands in front of The Cricketers Inn. Nash pushed his third delivery a little wider into the off side, but Sobers went down the wicket and drove it into the pavilion enclosure beyond the long-off boundary. Nash tried another variation by dropping the fourth ball a little shorter but Sobers rocked on to his back foot, and pulled it high over the scoreboard. The young bowler was still not disconcerted, even if the fielders seemed to be spreading further and further out, and he put the next delivery on a good length on the off stump. Sobers for once made a mistake and the ball travelled straight to Roger Davis on the long-off boundary. He caught it, but in so doing fell over the ropes, and after a consultation between the umpires, another six was signalled.

By now the crowd and the players alike were aware that the great West Indian all-rounder was on the verge of becoming the first player to hit six sixes in an over. As Nash regathered the ball and pondered on where to put the last delivery, Eifion Jones [the Glamorgan wicket-keeper] jokingly said to Sobers: 'Bet you can't hit this one for six as well.' The West Indian simply turned around and grinned, took guard and despatched the ball like a rocket out of the ground and down St Helen's Avenue. So hard did Sobers hit it, that the ball was not found until the next day.*

Sobers scored more than 1500 runs and took 84 wickets for Nottinghamshire in what was to be their best season of his residence; Majid topped 1300 runs for Glamorgan, and Asif Iqbal's entertaining strokeplay was a feature of Kent's challenge as they finished runners-up in the County Championship for the second successive summer. But pride of place among the newcomers went not to a Test cricketer but to a twenty-three-year-old blond-haired batsman from Natal, Barry Richards. Recruited by Hampshire after the West Indian Test batsman, Clive Lloyd, had turned them down in preference to a year's qualification period for Lancashire, Richards scored 2395 runs with batting so supreme, so sublime that it made wishful thinking of the Clark Report's hope that 'overseas star players will not only raise the standard of county teams by their individual prowess, but they should also have a beneficial effect on the young men who play with them'. Watching Barry Richards bat was a daunting experience for most aspiring cricketers, batsmen or bowlers, though one June morning in 1974 he did bring out the best in a young Somerset all-rounder called Ian Botham, who trimmed the South African's off bail when he had made only 13 in a Benson and Hedges quarter-final. As it happened, the batsman best placed to learn most from Richards,

* Andrew Hignell. *The History of Glamorgan County Cricket Club* (Christopher Helm, 1988)

his Hampshire opening partner Gordon Greenidge, chose to play for West Indies rather than England.

Despite the impact of the instant imports, however, the County Championship was won by the one county not currying foreign favours. Yorkshire's title in 1968 was their fourth since Brian Close took over the captaincy in 1963, their thirty-first in all, and it completed a hat-trick. But it was also their last for many years, and in 1992, having watched other counties mainline their way to trophies, they finally set aside their principles and signed their own overseas player. They needed a bowler, badly; they ended up with a batsman, the teenage Indian prodigy, Sachin Tendulkar. Well, that's how the market was. Even with the counties now restricted to just one overseas player, the demand for star names outstripped the supply, and Yorkshire's sponsors wanted a star. 'Yorkshire TV might as well run the club,' quipped the former England captain, Ray Illingworth, when the county replaced Tendulkar the following season with another big-name batsman in the West Indies captain, Richie Richardson.

The overseas players' great value to county cricket was as levellers. Their presence, plus the introduction of two more one-day competitions – the John Player Sunday League in 1969 and the Benson and Hedges Cup in 1972 – meant that more of the counties began to compete for honours; and the game benefited from the media interest generated throughout the country, rather than in one or two counties. In the West Country, Gloucestershire and Somerset threw off years of trials and tribulations to challenge for the Championship and put their names on the one-day trophies.

Mike Procter, the enthusiastic South African all-rounder, the languid Pakistani strokemaker, Zaheer Abbas, and his fellow-countryman, Sadiq Mohammad, youngest of the four Test-playing brothers, helped Gloucestershire win the Gillette Cup in 1973 and the Benson and Hedges Cup in 1977. Two outstanding West Indians, Viv Richards and Joel Garner, joined forces with Ian Botham to send Somerset's bucolic supporters to Lord's five times in six seasons from 1978, in addition to chanting them to the Sunday League title in 1979. Nottinghamshire, after a false dawn under Sobers, bought their place in the sun by hiring two lean,

laconic all-rounders in the South African Clive Rice and the New
Zealander Richard Hadlee. One on his own would have improved
Nottinghamshire's fortunes, but not to the extent that these two
complementary cricketers were able to by working in tandem.

The fact that Gloucestershire, for example, could field three
players ineligible for England provides an illustration of how
short-sighted the game's administrators can be. Indeed, however
well intentioned, in retrospect cricket's planning seems ridicu-
lously short-term, devised more for the moment than for the
future, failing to take into account man's determination to advantage himself of any loophole, rather than close it. When deciding
to introduce immediate registration, the counties agreed that an
overseas player, if resident in England for five years, would be
regarded in the same category as an English-born player. Five
years was nothing for cricketers who now had the opportunity of
playing all year round, in England and out of England. Eventually
this period of residence was extended to ten years, though in 1987,
when it looked as if its legislation might deprive the England
team of the prolific Zimbabwean run-scorer Graeme Hick,
the Test and County Cricket Board reduced the term to seven
years.

The immediate effect concerned not Hick, who still had several
years to wait, but Warwickshire's Alvin Kallicharran, who found
himself no longer an overseas player. The previous year the Board
had rejected his application to be regarded as 'English qualified'
on the grounds that insufficient time had passed since he last
played for West Indies in 1980. Judging from the expressions on
the faces of Board officials when this was pointed out to them by
the press, it is doubtful if Kallicharran's position had been part
of the debate when the shorter period of residence was discussed.

Although the presence of the overseas players helped counties in
their pursuit of honours, it did not solve an intrinsic problem of
the County Championship. In presenting a case for four-day Championship cricket, the Murray Report was critical of the way 'joke'
bowling had demeaned the professional game and, while accepting
that it had always played a part in rain-affected matches and

those between equally matched sides, it felt that such bowling had increased significantly in recent seasons.

While it is not easy to judge the degree of increase, contemporary records from the 1960s indicate that the prevalence of 'joke' bowling is by no means recent. 'Bunfights' was one description applied thirty years earlier to Championship games in which a hectic finish followed several days of purposeless cricket. '. . . the old fearful formula of two doleful days, followed by dodgy declarations and a blatant beer match,' A. A. Thomson wrote of them. The England and Sussex captain, Ted Dexter, claiming that England's players were 'not geared to five-day Tests', said that county cricket comprised a two-day struggle for first-innings points, after which the two captains made a tacit arrangement. And one correspondent to *The Cricketer* advocated the four-day Championship game as an antidote to 'the futile third day of county matches when a phoney finish is so often contrived'.

When I was editor of *Wisden*, I favoured four-day Championship matches, believing that the three-day game, as it was played, produced too many instances of meaningless cricket. What also worried me was whether there were enough players of sufficient quality in county cricket to set and maintain a consistently high standard among seventeen, now eighteen, counties. Now it really is up to the players to make four-day cricket work, because the working parties are beginning to run out of options. I wonder, sometimes, if the cricketers themselves realize this. Looking back at how often reforms have achieved the opposite of what was intended, one does wonder.

Defenders of the three-day game in the early 1990s linked their case to that for uncovered pitches in the County Championship. The Murray Report, however, believed that a return to uncovered pitches at international level was 'out of the question' for commercial reasons, and I recall Mike Gatting's comment, when he was England's captain, that there was no point in having uncovered pitches because Test cricket was played on covered pitches. When one sees the amount of time lost in Test cricket because of dubious light and damp patches at deep square leg, it is almost worth arguing that little more time would be lost by leaving the pitches open to the weather and telling the players and the umpires to get on with the game. Gatting's argument strikes me as having a reverse logic.

Recalling the excitement of cricket played on uncovered pitches is not sufficient reason, however, for their return. They produced better batsmen, of that I'm certain, and they gave spin bowlers a chance to come into their own. But the blue-remembered days were the days of adventurous amateur captains, and of bowling attacks balanced by fast bowling and spin. The days, too, when pitches were faster and harder than they have been since the sixties. Not even in the 1960s, it has to be remembered, when pitches were uncovered after an experimental period of covering, did spinners take undue precedence over seamers at the top of the national averages.

The glut of runs scored immediately after the Second World War prompted the authorities to ask for grassier pitches, which would restore the balance between bat and ball, and even before the war MCC had recommended that, in order to produce more sporting pitches, there should be less heavy rolling. By the early 1960s counties were preparing pitches with so much grass on them that Gubby Allen, in his year as president of MCC, felt it necessary to warn of the danger to cricket inherent in seam-dominated bowling. For 1964 the counties agreed that pitches should have less grass on them, and if possible should be much faster at the start of the game, a recurring theme if ever there was one. By the end of the summer, though, John Arlott was bemoaning that little good had come of the new instruction: '. . . by and large, the season's pitches were bad, particularly in view of all the fine weather we have had.' Not all the counties had complied with the instructions, going ahead instead with pitches that favoured their seam-oriented attacks. And even where the grass had been thinned out, the foundation of the pitch itself was often found wanting. In a little over a decade, irreparable damage had been done.

It affected not just the playing environment but, with the slowing of the over-rate which accompanied the emphasis on seam bowling, the game's momentum also. It didn't take long for captains to discover that seam-up line-and-length bowling gave away fewer runs and had a greater wicket-taking potential on the slow pitches of the day. Besides, it required less tactical imagination to put on two seam bowlers and wait for something to happen, which it often would on pitches of uneven bounce or lateral movement or sometimes both. Correspondingly, the batsmen were also waiting for something to happen and so were not willing to take unnecessary risks. Even on a damp or drying pitch, the spinner's happy hunting ground, captains often stuck with the seamers, preferring to see the ball fly from just short of a length than watch it turn and beguile. Besides, any lateral movement obtained by a seam bowler was sharper than the slow turn obtained by the spinner.

So it was argued, and the evidence of the averages supported the argument. Under cross-examination, however, the evidence did not always stand up. The England and Lancashire fast bowler, Brian Statham, took 100 or more wickets in a season thirteen times in his nineteen-year career, and from 1963 to 1966 he did so in successive seasons. But this most honest of cricketers never deluded himself about his Indian summer successes. 'The situation is ridiculous,' he said in 1965, when with 137 wickets at 12.52 apiece he was third in the national averages behind the Derbyshire pair, Harold Rhodes and Brian Jackson. 'After all the years I've been in cricket I'm not bowling any faster or showing any sudden great improvement at my age. I've bowled well, but the main reason for the results has been the atrocious wickets up and down the country.'*

Fourth in the averages that same season was Warwickshire's Tom Cartwright, with 108 wickets at 13.93. The year before he had taken 134 wickets at 15.97. In between, touring South Africa with MCC, he took twenty-five wickets at 32.68 in eight games – only Ian Thomson and the spinners, David Allen and Fred Titmus, bowled more overs – while his two wickets in his only Test match there cost 196 runs. In terms of runs per over he was economical, giving away fewer than two and a half in his Test match, and not much more than two in all matches. But, even allowing for his

* *The Cricketer*, November 1965

fitness problems in South Africa, his lack of penetration betrayed the extent to which he owed his success in England to the type of pitches prepared there. Micky Stewart struck exactly the right note when he wrote in *The Cricketer* in 1965 that 'Anyone who deliberately produces inferior wickets for their own selfish means is doing English cricket a great disservice.'

As with much of what Stewart has thought about cricket over the years, this made good sense, and too little notice was taken of it. By the mid-eighties, when bowlers capturing 100 wickets in a season were fewer than in the succulent sixties, Neal Radford's success on Worcester's green-tops (and many others around the circuit) had all but the *cognoscenti* calling for his inclusion in the England side. When the ball deviated this way and that he could be a handful, even if his 101 wickets at 24.68 in 1985 hardly bore witness to a Test-class bowler. And so it was proved: on a good pitch he looked ordinary in Test cricket, and his four wickets at 87.75 apiece adequately reflect the shortcomings of his three Test appearances.

Stewart and the England Committee knew only too well that if England were to have good bowlers they would first have to learn to bowl on good pitches: on the kind of pitch they would experience in Test cricket. It was 1990 before the counties produced pitches that no longer favoured bowlers, particularly the seam bowlers, and helped by a sunny summer the batsmen extracted a dreadful revenge, notching a record 428 individual hundreds. The pitches were pilloried; so was the England Committee. But as Machiavelli had forecast several centuries before, 'The innovator has for his enemies all those who would have done well under the old conditions.'

7

Barber or Boycott?

Pitches, or more pointedly the way they were prepared, were not the only factor in the swing away from spin bowling. Some of the experimental laws introduced by the Advisory Committee helped speed along the process, and in this respect 1957 was a particularly poor year, bringing into play standardized boundaries, bonus points for the team leading on first innings, provided they scored at a faster rate, and a limitation on the number of leg-side fieldsmen. Each, undoubtedly, was the result of good intentions, if not in every instance of good intelligence. Put together, they changed the way first-class cricket in England was played.

It was hoped that limiting the boundaries in county cricket to seventy-five yards, from the middle of the pitch, would improve the tempo of the game by encouraging batsmen to hit more sixes and fours. But this was nullified by the reaction of many captains to the introduction of bonus points. The thinking behind these was that they would quicken the tempo of a game in its early stages. Instead the cricketer, being a contrary beast as well as a conservative one, responded by seeking ways of preventing batsmen from scoring quickly. Containing bowling became the norm, years in advance of limited-overs cricket, which in due course was blamed for the emphasis on defensive bowling. By the time one-day cricket came on the county scene the containing line-and-length seamer was well in the groove and the spinner was already feeling the chilly winds of redundancy.

After all, it made sense tactically. Captains cautious in the extreme when it came to allowing their opponents a few bonus points were not going to concede runs by having spin bowlers thumped to the shorter boundaries. A double blow for the spinners, especially for the off-spinners, was the limitation of on-side fieldsmen to five, with no more than two men behind the popping crease. Initially introduced to curb fast and medium-pace bowlers who consistently slanted their attack into the leg stump, this restriction firstly deprived the off-spinner of a field to support his spin on a 'turner', and secondly encouraged batsmen to hit to the on side, even from outside the off stump. A game whose glories were painted in 'open' off-side strokes became a 'closed' push and prod, tip and tuck affair for no better reason than ill-judged legislation.

Ill-judged would be a harsh verdict if made only with the benefit of hindsight, but the counties themselves were aware after just one season that the on-side limitation militated against off-spin bowlers; yet they continued with the experiment not for just one more season but until November 1965. Their one concession to cricketing sense had come right at the beginning when they substituted the words 'behind the popping crease' for 'behind the wicket', with regard to the two-men-behind limitation. This aspect of the law remains in force today, as I know from personal experience, having transgressed it one dreamy afternoon in the shadow of the Sussex Downs.

Always in conflict was the desire of the authorities to make cricket an entertaining game, which they hoped would bring back the spectators, and the attitude of the players. At the end of 1957, the captains voted the seventy-five-yard boundary a great success; but then they would have, seeing it only from a playing point of view. Not so far to run in the field; no conceding five runs while a 'Bomber' Wells made his way to third man in pursuit of an edge that was not worth a single – though I seem to think they moved 'Bomber' out of the slips soon after that. It was the kind of thing the crowds loved, though. It was much more fun than watching a batsman forever working the ball off his legs through mid-wicket.

Fun, however, was not what the game was about any longer, or so it seemed. Captains were encouraged more and more to make the game entertaining, and more and more they concentrated on dull, often negative tactics. It is worth noting that MCC, in appointing the England and Warwickshire captain, M. J. K. Smith, to lead its side to Australia in 1965–66, asked him if he was prepared to follow a policy of positive cricket. Interesting, too, that the tour manager, Billy Griffith, the MCC secretary, is reported to have said he was not prepared to take on that role unless this was the policy. 'People overseas expect to see cricket played on the right lines,' said the chairman of selectors, Doug Insole. 'Griffith's job will be to see that England do this.' Griffith himself said that he would ask Smith to take action 'if we find things slipping a bit, as they did in Sydney during the last tour'.

For much of the 1965–66 tour of Australia, the team's enterprise was widely acclaimed, and after their innings victory in the Third Test at Sydney hopes were high that they would bring back the Ashes. In the event, a non-first-class fixture against Northern New South Wales and two games in Tasmania were not what MCC needed to keep on the boil; the Australians came back to win at Adelaide by an innings and square the series. The final Test was something of an anticlimax, drawn after the loss of the fourth day, yet it had moments which encapsulated the tour. Ken Barrington showed the value of an attacking policy by reaching his century from 122 balls, inside two and a half hours. But in the field England averaged twelve eight-ball overs an hour (the equivalent of sixteen six-ball overs) and that earlier momentum was lost. 'On one score – one that is vital to the health of the game – Smith must be roundly condemned,' says *Wisden*. 'He did little, if anything, to stir dawdling bowlers and fielders to maintain a satisfactory over rate.' Today, of course, with the ICC minimum of fifteen overs an hour, Smith's attack would be one over in credit.

A more technical criticism of Smith's captaincy in the field was his handling of the spin bowlers. As they had in the series in South Africa the previous winter, also under Smith, Allen and Titmus bowled the most overs, but their wickets were expensive, and as they came at an average of 121 and 187 balls respectively, their bowling was hardly penetrative. Allen was the more attacking of the two; Titmus, with a flatter, more defensive trajectory, was often preferred. Little opportunity was taken throughout the tour to make something of the leg-spinning ability of Barber or Barrington, bringing to mind the unadventurous use of the Essex leg-spinner, Robin Hobbs, in South Africa. Hobbs, if I'm right, was on call in each of the five Tests as twelfth man because of his outstanding fielding. His absence from the Test side reflected not simply the attitude of one English captain to spin bowling, particularly leg-spin bowling, but of many county captains towards spin bowling in general when seam was allowed to prevail in the domestic first-class game.

MCC's reputation for enterprising play on that 1965–66 tour of Australia was built on their batting, and in particular on the performances of the thirty-year-old left-handed opener Bob Barber. Tall and powerfully built, he attacked from the start with a cavalier spirit which quickly won him the admiration of Australian crowds and the respect of their cricketers. The apogee of his tour, on which he scored 1001 runs for an average of 50.05, was his magnificently aggressive 185 in the Third Test, made in 296 minutes, off 255 balls, with nineteen fours. Listeners to the commentary from the Sydney Cricket Ground were as spellbound as those watching as England's two 'Bs', Barber and Boycott, having put on 93 off twenty-six overs in the two hours before lunch, stepped up the rate to add another 141 in the first two hours of the afternoon. When Barber was second out, England had 303 on the board, John Edrich was bound for his second hundred in successive Test innings, and England were set to record their first innings victory over Australia, in Australia, since 1936–37. So severe was Barber's assault on Australia's opening bowlers that Graham McKenzie, none for 113, was left out of the side for the Adelaide Test, only to be recalled when the Queensland fast bowler Peter Allan was unfit. As is the way of such things in cricket, McKenzie celebrated his reprieve by bowling Barber for a duck.

I think it was Edrich who said he learned to bat overseas, on good pitches. Certainly nothing Barber managed in his eleven Tests in England compared with what he achieved in Australia and South Africa, but it is hard to believe, some twenty-five years later, that he played for England only three more times after that Ashes series: in the Fourth and Fifth Tests against the 1966 West Indians, and in the First Test against Australia in 1968. However, on his return from Australia in 1966 he played county cricket on a part-time basis only, in order to give more time to the family business. Indeed, he played just eleven first-class games for Warwickshire that season, as well as helping them win the Gillette Cup, and it took the England selectors – not to mention Warwickshire's supporters – some time to come to terms with such individualism. With a half-century in the Championship and a century in the Gillette Cup in successive matches against Gloucestershire in June, he showed no signs of suffering from his absence. Cyril Washbrook, the Man of the Match adjudicator for the Gillette Cup tie at Edgbaston, ranked Barber's electrifying 113 against Gloucestershire, with its seventeen boundaries, as the best innings he had seen in the competition. Such was his dominance that Warwickshire went from 50 to 100 in nine overs, and from 100 to 150 in six. By the time the England selectors brought him back in August, however, batting on under-prepared pitches in county cricket had begun to affect the standards of personal performance he set himself.

Knowing he was not dependent on cricket for his livelihood must have helped Barber to bat with such freedom. But he was not always so flamboyant. Of his first season at Edgbaston, in 1963, *Wisden* recorded that 'Barber brought a touch of northern dourness to the batting' and was more expansive about his leg-spinners, which 'introduced much-needed variety into the bowling ... He provided several finishing touches and did the hat-trick against Glamorgan.' The northern dourness was a reference to Barber's time at Lancashire, for whom he had appeared as a schoolboy before going to Cambridge, and whom he captained in 1960 and 1961.

The turning-point came in 1964, when Warwickshire promoted him to open the batting, and among his three centuries for them that season was one before lunch against the Australians. His 138, made out of 209 before he was second out, took him two and a quarter hours and gave the tourists some warning of what was in store for them in 1965–66. John Woodcock, reviewing the 1964 season for *The Cricketer*, noted that 'Barber's transformation from a dull and stodgy batsman to a carefree and attractive opener dates from a one-day knockout match when he discovered the joy and the rewards of throwing the bat'. In that Gillette Cup innings, at Northampton, Barber hit 114, including eighteen boundaries, and as with most of his attacking innings a high proportion of his runs came from gloriously struck strokes through the covers. Medium-pace bowlers, used to containing the batsmen by bowling just short of a length, had to readjust their sights when Barber moved out of the crease to hit them.

The Gillette Cup sent Geoff Boycott to Australia in an attacking frame of mind, too. His 146 for Yorkshire against Surrey in the 1965 final, containing three sixes and fifteen fours, remains one of the outstanding innings of the competition, as well as a salient feature of the Boycott enigma. He, like Barber, used his feet against the quicker bowlers to drive them straight, and when they dropped short he played that forcing stroke past point which became his trademark. This, gathered Woodcock at the time, was how Boycott played 'until he was affected by the awful seriousness of first-class cricket' – and for Boycott in 1965, first-class cricket had been not only awfully serious but seriously awful. He did not hit one first-class hundred all season.

To what extent his century at Lord's was roses all the way remains a matter for conjecture, as Derek Hodgson discovered when writing the official history of Yorkshire.

> According to Close the opening pair of Taylor and Boycott had become so bogged down by the Surrey seam attack that he, the captain, went in at three to move things along and told Boycott first to start looking for singles, then to put some force into his shots and finally to 'hit everything'. According to Boycott, his mid-wicket conversation with Close, on the captain's arrival, concerned details as to who was bowling well and who was to be attacked. The extreme version of the story, unconfirmed but part of the legend, is that Close threatened to run out Boycott unless he accelerated.*

* Derek Hodgson. *The Official History of Yorkshire County Cricket Club* (The Crowood Press, 1989)

By the end of the 1965–66 tour of Australia, though, the other side of Boycott had prevailed. Opening with Barber in the final Test, which England had to win to regain the Ashes, he took sixty of the first eighty balls bowled, scoring just 15 runs, and off the last ball of the eleventh over he ran out Barber in trying to keep the strike. It was a terrible call for a ridiculous run. Still, as Boycott's run-outs went, it will figure lower down the list than that which sent poor Derek Randall slowly and sadly back to the Trent Bridge pavilion in July 1977. That was a clanger of the first order.

The match had all the elements of a highly charged drama without needing another one. For a start, it marked Boycott's return to Test cricket after three years of self-imposed exile, and on the first day the gates were closed before lunch at Trent Bridge for the first time since Bradman's Australians played there in 1948. More importantly for the Nottinghamshire supporters, it was the first Test appearance on his home ground for Derek Randall, the madcap hero of Melbourne the previous March, when he made his memorable 174 in the Centenary Test. Twice that summer, at Lord's and Manchester, he had passed fifty against Australia; now, at Trent Bridge, the gods and the Gunns waited for the century that would seal his triumph. They were to wait in vain.

Randall had scored 13 runs in his inimitably exhilarating fashion when Boycott, having no more than pushed the ball back down the pitch, set off for an impossible single. Randall, backing up, could have safely regained his ground, but instead he chose to run, thus sacrificing his wicket. As wicket-keeper Marsh pole-axed the middle and off stumps with a roundhouse right, Boycott covered his face with his hands, a figure of dejection no less tragic than that of his departing partner. He soon lost Greig and Miller, and when joined by Alan Knott he had been batting three hours for no more than 20 runs. England were 82 for five, and the black cap Boycott wore again with such pride might have been to pronounce his own sentence. When within minutes he edged Pascoe to McCosker, it seemed as if he had; when McCosker, at second slip, dropped the catch, all of England breathed a sigh of relief and simultaneously wondered if there was such a thing as justice.

Bad light ended play half an hour early that day, with Boycott 88 not out; he had been batting since the evening before. Knott, the saviour of the innings with an impudent display which gradually restored Boycott's confidence and lifted England's morale, was 87 not out, and deservedly he reached his hundred first on Saturday. Boycott finally achieved his, having batted for six hours and eighteen minutes. It was neither heroic nor historic – that came next at Headingley – but it helped to put England in charge. On Tuesday Randall made the winning hit, and as he and Boycott, 80 not out, walked off arm in arm, the run-out had been forgiven and forgotten.

The gates were closed once more before the start of the Fourth Test at Headingley, where a great crowd gathered to acclaim what would be Boycott's 100th hundred. 'They sat devotedly – almost devoutly – thickly massed all day under blazing sun'* and he did not let them down. He didn't let himself down. By the close he was unbeaten with 110, the first of the eighteen centurions to reach this landmark in a Test. Next day he batted England into an impregnable position, and when at last he went – last man out for 191 – he had been at the crease for a minute under ten and a half hours. Since his return to Test cricket, in fact, he had tormented the Australian bowlers for twenty-two and a half hours in three innings.

There were times, I have to admit it, when it intrigued me to watch Boycott bat. He was no flash Harry, all dash and dart; his craftsmanship was consummative. In a Habitat age which wanted style it could throw away tomorrow, Boycott built innings that were meant to last. He was a technician at a time when no one served apprenticeships, and subsequent generations struggled to remember what Britain had lost. True, he bored the pants off men with memories of Hammond cover-driving sequence upon sequence of half-volleys to far-flung corners, but Boycott was never magisterial in that manner. So self-centred that he drove his colleagues, his critics and even his friends to distraction, he was none the less his own man, and to his own self he remained true. I have

---

* John Arlott in the *Guardian*, 12 August 1977

often thought that if Boycott scored his hundred, however selfishly, and the other ten averaged twenty each before he ran them out, that would be 300 on the board. As always happens, though, some among the other ten wanted a share of the glory. Boycott was an exception, and ordinary men can't live in the shadow of exceptions. Even politicians discover that.

8

Free Spirit in an Oval Cage

In 1971 Geoffrey Boycott became the first Englishman to finish an English season with a batting average of 100. Previously only two Australians had managed this distinction: Don Bradman in 1938 and Bill Johnston in 1953. Johnston's average and aggregate, it should perhaps be added, were a complementary 102, being achieved by sixteen not out innings in seventeen visits to the crease. Boycott's aggregate of 2503 runs contained thirteen hundreds, and in only four innings did he fail to reach double figures. It is not surprising that Tony Lewis, appraising the season for *The Cricketer*, admitted that his main recollection from it would be of Boycott 'playing the full range of his strokes with deadly efficiency. No lasting poetry perhaps in the roll of the wrists or the flow of the bat, but one was left in awe by his perfect selection of strokes – a brilliant craftsman taking out highly polished tools specified for different jobs and neatly replacing them, ball by ball.' Yet Yorkshire, whom Boycott was captaining for the first time, experienced the worst season in their long, proud history, finishing thirteenth in the Championship after going seventeen first-class games without a win – the longest sequence of this kind they had suffered. In the Sunday League they finished fifteenth, and they were knocked out of the Gillette Cup, by Kent, in their first game.

Champions that summer, as we saw in an earlier chapter, were Micky Stewart's Surrey, and hard on the heels of their success The Oval was packed by a capacity crowd estimated at more than 31,000. The crowd was not there, sad to say, to celebrate Surrey's summer, but for a rock concert to aid the Bangladesh appeal fund for refugees from the civil war in East Pakistan. Topping the bill were one of the great bands of their time, The Who, whose lead guitarist, Pete Townshend, interspersed high jumps and guitar-smashing with his own brand of hard-driving rock and roll like a leg-spinner going through his repertoire of leg-spin, top-spin, googlies and frenzied appeals. But as Who fans roared approvingly at Townshend's antics and his playing, to one side of the stage, figuratively if not literally out of the spotlight, almost motionless, stood the band's bass player, John Entwistle, rather like Boycott a craftsman taking out highly polished tools for different jobs and replacing them, note by note.

If Boycott could have been more like John Entwistle, the focus of a devoted following that was drawn by his technique rather than by a personality cult, his and Yorkshire's story would have been a less traumatic one. But Boycott didn't want to be John Entwistle; he wanted to be Pete Townshend, the leader of the band. What he would not have understood, and what his supporters never seemed to understand, is that Boycott wasn't born to follow. If Pete Townshend had been like Geoffrey Boycott, The Who would have gone down like a lead balloon. It had nothing to do with technique; it had everything to do with chemistry; to do with fusion.

Cricket's great need was not someone who would go down like a lead balloon. It needed someone who would take off like a Led Zeppelin, and it found him in Ian Botham. For just as Jimmy Page, Led Zep's guitarist, could lead his band down heavy rock roads or up quiet stairways, so Botham possessed the technical ability and the temperament to play as a situation demanded. Not only could he batter and bash with the best of them: he was the best of them. With the ball he swept aside opposition batsmen with audacious deliveries in riff-like sequences. How did it go at Edgbaston in 1981? Five Australian wickets for one run in twenty-eight deliveries. That was show-stopping in the Jimi Hendrix class, and he'd been dead more than a decade. Yet when it was important, Botham could play tight, controlled chords until the time was right to soar into a solo.

He played like that against Australia at Old Trafford in 1981.

Coming to the wicket when England in their second innings were 104 for five, a lead of 205 with more than two days remaining, he spent seventy minutes scoring just 28 runs and then exploded in such a way that his innings of 118 took only 123 minutes. Of the eighty-six balls he needed to reach three figures, fifty-three were used in that first seventy minutes of reconnaissance. In eight overs against the bowling of Lillee and Alderman with the new ball Botham hit 66 runs, including three hooked sixes off Lillee and a huge pull off Alderman which ended up way back in the crowd; his final tally of six sixes was a record for an Ashes Test. He also hit thirteen fours, and the power and cleanness of his hitting earned him deserved comparison with the legendary Gilbert Jessop. Not even the legendary Buddy Guy could have blown away a crowd of 20,000 as sensationally as Botham did that summer Saturday at Manchester.

Adorning the same stage as Botham from the late seventies into the early nineties was another favourite of the crowds, David Gower, a left-hander like Hendrix but in performance more like Jimmy Page's erstwhile Yardbird contemporary Eric Clapton: laid-back, mellow and magnificent. No graffiti at Lord's heralded 'Gower is God', but from a June day at Edgbaston in 1978, when the golden-haired twenty-one-year-old nonchalantly pulled his first ball in Test cricket for four, they could have. Gower that day gave his partner, Clive Radley, a hundred-minute start and with a string of cultured strokes caught him up in the fifties. He was then out to what *Wisden* called an 'uncharacteristic, wild swing'. Well, how was *Wisden* to know that this was how this mighty was inclined to fall. Before the fall, though, Gower was as compulsive watching as Clapton was compulsive listening (and watching). Each played on a different plane from his peers; each at times looked as if he was living there as well. Neither moved his feet much, but the beauty of what they produced pushed how they did it into the background. It was more than style, it was more than talent. Each put his signature on what he did and that lived in the memory of all who witnessed it.

Not that Gower lacked technique. It is simply that his batting transgressed technique in a way that Boycott's, for example, rarely did. Yet if Boycott had played with Gower's freedom, and Gower had played with Boycott's resolution, which of them, it is interesting to speculate, would appear at the top of England's run-makers? When he was recalled to the England team during the 1992 series against Pakistan, Gower in his first Test match for seventeen months overhauled both Boycott's record England aggregate of 8114 runs and Sir Colin Cowdrey's record of 114 Tests for England. By the end of the series Gower had improved his record to 8231 runs, average 44.25, from 204 innings in 117 Tests. Boycott, average 47.72, played 193 innings in 108 Tests.

Whereas Boycott was something of an enigma for English cricket throughout his career, Gower in his later years has posed something of a conundrum. For many, Boycott was beyond comprehension; for a few, Gower wasn't worth comprehending. Of the two, I suspect that Gower made more of an effort to accommodate his critics, but while this won him many sympathizers, it won him few favours.

Gower was a natural; a free spirit who in his prime saw the ball early and whose first instinct was to score from it. A graceful style came as easily to him as it did to Sobers, but like all cricketers he was subject to technical problems which could not always be sorted out in the middle. Even genius requires practice, as Sobers discovered at times. 'The nets had been foreign soil to him previously,' Jack Fingleton wrote, when he recalled the half-hour's net practice Sobers took prior to his superlative innings of 254 for the Rest of the World against Australia at Melbourne in 1971–72. Sir Donald Bradman called it 'probably the greatest exhibition of batting ever seen in Australia'.

Australians who have seen some of Gower's finest innings cannot imagine how England have come to regard him as anything but an automatic selection. In 42 Tests against them, between 1978–79 and 1990–91, he batted to par, averaging 44.78 to his career Test average of 44.25. Hutton (56.46/56.67) and Boycott (47.50/47.72) did the same. Barrington averaged 63.96 in Ashes Tests against a career average of 58.67, and John Edrich 48.96 against 43.54, but Cowdrey managed only 34.26 against Australia compared with 44.06 in all Tests. Indeed, only Sir Donald

Bradman and Sir Jack Hobbs have scored more runs than Gower in Ashes Tests; and just in case someone says, 'Ah, but how many more Tests did Gower play?' the answer is one more than Hobbs and five more than Bradman.

After Gower's first tour of Australia, with Mike Brearley's side in 1978–79, the captain described him as 'a minor genius who may become a major genius'. But if Goethe is to be believed, genius develops in quiet places, and Gower was not one for quiet places. He flowered in the big time, but in opening his petals he sometimes exposed his faults – sometimes, to the frustration of even his admirers, the same faults. It is character, according to Goethe, that develops in the full current of human life, and I have wondered if Gower's 'minor genius' has not at times been mistaken for character; style being confused with content. There was content, but it was in the runs he scored.

What Gower always possessed was that precious gift of timing which raised his game above that of his contemporaries. It did not raise it necessarily in terms of runs on the board but in the effort-less way he acquired them. It was a different game when Gower was batting, as it was when Colin Cowdrey was on song. But there was a difference between these two great timers of the ball. When Cowdrey's timing deserted him he could look almost ordi-nary, unable to hit the ball off the square until the priceless gift returned. When Gower's timing deserted him he was never at the crease long enough to look ordinary. He rarely stayed around, waiting for his timing to return. *Du sublime au ridicule il n'y a qu'un pas*, was often Gower's Napoleonic code.

It was noted on Gower's first tour of Australia that technically he had 'some faults to iron out', and back in Australia a year later, with Dennis Lillee in particular moving the ball in and away from him at will, his stroke selection and his footwork were found wanting. 'Nobody would wish to curb his attacking bent,' Peter Smith wrote for *Wisden*, 'but the tour management was entitled to demand a more responsible selection of strokes than those that resulted in his dismissal when England were already deep in trouble.' Eleven years later, *Wisden*'s account of the Adelaide Test reports how 'Gower, obligingly chipping the last ball of the morning to long leg, one of three men positioned for the stroke, ushered in a collapse . . .' This dismissal followed the infamous prank during the Queensland match at Carrara, when Gower and the Derbyshire batsman John Morris buzzed the ground in Tiger Moth aircraft to acknowledge Robin Smith's hundred. As well as the management's displeasure, it earned them each a fine of £1000, and in Gower's case that incident, combined with his dismissal at Adelaide, struck from the management's memory the magnificent hundreds with which he entranced the crowds at Melbourne and Sydney in the previous two Tests.

If there is something in Swift's proposition that 'Censure is the tax a man pays to the public for being eminent,' the outcry which greeted Gower's omission from the England team to tour India and Sri Lanka in 1992–93 suggested that the public felt Gower deserved a tax rebate. Whether that sternest of critics, Bill O'Reilly, would have agreed is another matter. Garry Sobers, he claimed during West Indies' tour of Australia in 1960–61, 'forgot that a man with such a reputation is expected to adapt his programme to his team's benefit'. In other words, talents are not given to man for his own glorification or amusement; they are given to be used on behalf of his fellow-men, a precept one would have expected from an old-school Catholic like O'Reilly.

It is a philosophy to which England's captain, Graham Gooch, and manager, Micky Stewart, subscribed. Their critics spoke dismissively of 'work ethic mentality' and of subjugation of flair for commitment to the team. But the critics were missing a point, and ignoring a precedent. 'If you have great talents,' Sir Joshua Reynolds told students at the Royal Academy, 'industry will improve them: if you have but moderate abilities, industry will supply their deficiency.' The precedent? On Gower's first tour of Australia in 1978–79, we read in *Wisden*, 'Not a detail was left to chance. The day began with Barrington phoning every player with precise instructions – his expected dress, time of departure to the ground, and so on. Before play or net sessions Thomas [the England physiotherapist] organized PT and limbering-up exercises. Never has a touring party been so devoted to physical fitness and pre-breakfast runs in neighbouring parks.'

Had Barrington not died as the result of a heart attack during the Barbados Test in March 1981, the story of English cricket in the 1980s and the career of David Gower could have been different. Much loved by the players, a friend to all of them, Barrington brought with his personal dedication to the game, and to England, a sense of humour and a sense of fun not always on show to those outside the ring when he was batting single-mindedly in Surrey's or England's cause. Would Gooch, for one, and John Emburey, for another, have gone to South Africa as 'rebels' in 1981–82 had Barrington been in India that winter to advise them? And would Gower not have been reminded how, against Australia in December 1978 and against West Indies in April 1981, he had reined in his natural impulses, his flair, for his team's benefit?

At Perth in 1978, joining Boycott at the crease when England were 41 for three in overcast conditions which aided Australia's fast bowlers, Gower batted for four and a quarter hours for his 102. At Kingston in 1981, he earned England a draw in the final Test of that sad, troubled tour by batting through seven and three-quarter hours for an unbeaten 154. For *Wisden* Michael Melford noted that 'If he was still out to the loose or casual stroke, he now seldom succumbed to the wildly irrational one,' and his Test average for the series of 53.71 – against a West Indies attack comprising Holding, Garner, Roberts and Croft – was bettered only by Gooch's 57.50. At times on that tour Gooch batted with a rare brilliance which only emphasizes England's loss during his three years' suspension after the South African venture. In the second innings at Bridgetown he batted defiantly until eighth out for 116; in the first innings at Kingston he scored 153 of England's 249 for five by the 68th over, having reached 103 out of 155 in the fortieth over.

When England next toured the Caribbean, in 1985–86 and 1989–90, first Gower and then Gooch were captaining them. But the circumstances could hardly have been more different. England lost all five Tests on the first of those tours, with Gower no more capable of raising the morale of his side than he had been in 1984, his first full series as England captain, when West Indies also won all five Tests – the first of the so-called 'blackwashes'. On the

1989–90 tour, with Gooch as captain, Stewart as team manager and Gower in the press box, England won the First Test and should have won the Third but for the weather and time-wasting by the West Indians on the run-in to the tape. Having lost Gooch with a hand injury in that match, and subsequently for the rest of the series, they then lost the next two Tests under Allan Lamb, a vice-captain ill-equipped for promotion in the field. However, Gooch's stock could not have been higher, and the detailed attention to practice and preparation, pioneered by Barrington in Australia more than a decade earlier, was fully justified, if not fully accepted in every corner of the land.

Such professionalism was alien to the dilettantism which continued to bedevil so much of English life. It had not been so necessary in previous decades, and critics refused to see the need for it now. 'I bloody well wouldn't work here!' Fred Trueman said as he drove past a Jamaican sugar plantation with a sign extolling the virtues of 'Work, Obedience, Discipline'. Even his phlegmatic opening partner Brian Statham was moved to exclaim, 'This is too much like regimentation', after some heavy briefing on one MCC tour of Australia. But Trueman and Statham, like their fellow-professionals, knew what was expected of them, and when hard work was called for, hard work was given. It wasn't that Statham opposed regimentation; it was an insult for someone to think it might have been necessary for a professional cricketer. He had served his apprenticeship, he was a master of his trade.

If, in their day, the captain had chosen not to play in the opening game of a tour, had gone sailing instead, as Gower did in the West Indies in 1985–86, the professionals would have shrugged their shoulders, watched his sails dip over the horizon and got down to the business in hand. That was their business. But in Gower's side there were no professionals, only cricketers, and the captain was just another cricketer like them. True, he was a most gifted player, and they liked him. When it came to practice, though, he could not impose discipline on the side because he could not discipline himself to practise, even to set an example. Nor was he helped by the aversion to net practice of Ian Botham, a former England captain and a senior member of the side.

This is not to lay all the blame on Gower's shoulders. 'The winds and waves are always on the side of the ablest navigator,'* and Gower was not the luckiest of sailors that unhappy spring. His mother had died within a fortnight of the team's departure for the West Indies, and early into the tour he lost his pilot and vice-captain, Mike Gatting. Gatting's nose was broken when he edged a Malcolm Marshall delivery into his face during the first one-day international at Kingston. As if that wasn't sufficient misfortune, within twenty-four hours of Gatting's return to the West Indies after a three-week recuperation in England his thumb was broken. Consequently the player possessing the bulldog spirit that the side so desperately needed missed all but the final Test. Gatting owed his resurgent Test career to Gower's insistence that he be his vice-captain on England's tour of India in 1984–85, and he repaid Gower's faith in him by providing a bristling assertiveness which complemented Gower's less dynamic style of leadership. The series in India was won, and at home that summer England beat Australia convincingly to regain the Ashes. But without Gatting's drive, Gower's captaincy stalled and spiralled out of control. A more positive management pairing than Tony Brown and Bob Willis might have arrested the slide, but the record shows it was beyond their powers.

In its way, Gower's captaincy was as much the victim of his amiable personality as Colin Cowdrey's was. Being such a good player himself, he understood that cricketers have good and bad days, and when they failed they had his sympathy. 'You know just how fine the margin is,' Cowdrey once said. 'I don't storm up and down a dressing-room and say you must have been an idiot to play a shot like that at a time like that. When I come off the field, I know better than anyone whether I've played a bad shot. It wouldn't amuse me at all to have someone making several fairly classic statements of the obvious.' A sympathetic approach, unhappily, has never been enough when national teams lose. The press and the public want a triumph or a sacrifice, and as a rule they are rarely satisfied until they've been given the captain's head

---

* Edward Gibbon. *Decline and Fall of the Roman Empire* (1788)

on a plate. Gower's came garnished with Branston Pickle.

It is irony enough that when Gower's head rolled it was Gatting who took his place as England's captain. But there is a greater irony in the fact that Gower, who resurrected Gatting's Test career, once saved another successor, Graham Gooch, from a decision that could have damaged his international career. Gooch, who took over as vice-captain in the West Indies in 1986 when Gatting was injured, was personally disturbed – some might say unduly disturbed – by protests in the West Indian press, and at some grounds, aimed at the four England players in the side who had gone to South Africa in 1981–82. This had an adverse effect both on his cricket and on the mood of a team containing a number of players inclined towards defensive postures in the face of criticism. When the deputy prime minister of Antigua, Lester Bird, got in on the act, writing an unnecessarily derogatory article – though necessary, perhaps, for a politician – Gooch was ready to go home rather than travel to Antigua for the final Test. The secretary of the Test and County Cricket Board, Donald Carr, flew to Trinidad to persuade Gooch to change his mind, but it was Gower, appealing to Gooch's sense of loyalty, who was the more decisive influence.

When Gower's second chance at the England captaincy ended with the loss of the Ashes in 1989, his replacement was Gooch. And to add to the irony and the injury, when Gower was left out of the England side to tour India and Sri Lanka in 1992–93, under Gooch, the ostensible reason was that, with the selection of Gatting and Emburey, the team already contained enough older players. This was irrelevant nonsense, of course. Gower and Gatting were both thirty-five: Gower's Test average, as we have seen, was 44.25; Gatting's was 37.57 and he had been out of international cricket for three years, owing to the ban imposed after he had taken a side to South Africa in 1989–90. Had it not been for South Africa's readmission to the International Cricket Council in 1991, that ban would still have been in force and some other excuse would have had to be found for Gower's omission.

If age really had been a criterion, Gatting's inclusion ahead of Gower suggested that the England Committee saw Gatting as an

England player over a longer term than it saw Gower. Assuming that was the case, then one may wonder in what capacity. At the time of the tour to India and Sri Lanka, Alec Stewart, son of the recently retired England team manager, was heir apparent to Gooch, being his vice-captain. Indeed, it was announced that he would captain the side on the latter leg of the tour after Gooch returned home. But if Gatting were to regain his England Test place, and consolidate his position during the Ashes series of 1993, might the England Committee not think that the time had come to overlook his past indiscretions and appoint him in succession to Gooch for the tour of the West Indies in 1993–94?

Such a scenario could not have been written for Gower. He had not halted a Test match by an unseemly, not to mention untimely, confrontation with an umpire; he had not been bushwhacked by the tabloid newspapers for conduct unbecoming of an England captain (getting caught); he had not slunk off to South Africa, pocketing the rebel's rand, in contravention of ICC legislation. True, Gower lost England the Ashes, but it would have helped if Gooch had averaged more than 20.33 in that series, if Gatting had been available for more than one Test, and if even one of his main bowlers had been able to average under 35. The real truth, so it seemed to most people, was that Gower no longer fitted into the England Committee's frame of mind. Not on tour anyway. His dislike of limited-overs cricket was well known – he had admitted it often enough – and modern tours no longer just accommodated one-day internationals, they gave them the best room in the house. The one-day games were the crowd-pullers, the money-spinners. Then there was the premise that Gower could no longer be expected to conform: he could be a disruptive influence on the team spirit that was rated as so important to the bonding of a winning team. He might want to go off on his own for a few days, as he had on other tours, leaving lesser mortals miffed that they weren't entitled to such preferential treatment.

'Cricket,' wrote George Orwell, '. . . gives expression to a well-marked trait in the English character, the tendency to value "form" and "style" more highly than success. In the eyes of any true cricket-lover it is possible for an innings of 10 runs to be "better" (i.e., more elegant) than an innings of 100 runs . . .' In the eyes of the true cricket-lover that still applied, but as far as the England team was concerned, Orwell by the 1990s had passed his sell-by date. For them victory was important, not just in itself but as a tool to help the men marketing the game. A successful England team projected the right image, and on that image hung the financial welfare of English first-class cricket. So Gower's omission was not simply a victory for the new age of puritanism; it was also a symbol of the new age of pragmatism; of practicalism.

It seemed a long way from the time when MCC sent its secretary to Australia with M. J. K. Smith's team to ensure positive cricket. 'People overseas expect to see cricket played on the right lines,' Doug Insole had said at the time. What those lines were in the winter of 1992–93, when as chairman of Essex and of the TCCB International Committee Insole bade *bon voyage* to his county's captain, Gooch, and their former captain and coach, Keith Fletcher, was a matter of conjecture.

9

Uncivil Servants

The lines along which the England team play their cricket have long been a dilemma for players, captains, critics and selectors. They all want a victory, and when it is won, more often than not the result is allowed to justify the means. Test cricket is accepted as a serious matter. It is when the match or series is drawn or lost that the means are questioned, and the cry for entertaining cricket is renewed.

Dexter's final series as captain of England, the 1964 series against Australia, was roundly condemned as a dull affair, with both sides blamed for placing undue emphasis on a determination not to lose. England were not helped by an unsettled selection policy which gave their players little confidence to go on the attack; Australia employed an uncompromisingly defensive strategy to make the most of their available talents. Yet both teams found support from Raymond Robertson-Glasgow, the much loved 'Crusoe', one of the most entertaining writers on cricket and cricketers. While a classical scholar at Oxford, he won a Blue from 1920 to 1923, and he played for Somerset with varying frequency between 1920 and 1935, during which time he turned out five times for the Gentlemen against the Players.

Robertson-Glasgow enjoyed the Test matches between England and Australia in 1964. 'There have been better Tests and better players: and there have been worse,' he wrote in *The Cricketer* that autumn. 'But the point is, they *were* Tests: and *as* Tests, what mattered most of all to the players and most of the spectators was which side won. It is humbug to pretend otherwise. After the rainy end of the Fifth Test, at The Oval, my good friend, Denis Compton, in a most interesting TV talk, remarked that Test cricketers are "public entertainers". I'm afraid not. In hard fact, they are there primarily to hold or win the Ashes, somehow; not to entertain the public. What entertains and draws the public is the fact that it *is* a Test match; and these spectators don't mind slow play if it's done, even mistakenly, for The Cause; just as Yorkshiremen used once to take Lancashire's Harry Makepeace ("no fours before lunch") for granted. He wasn't there for fun. He was batting for The Cause.'

This is not to say that The Cause and entertaining cricket are incompatible. Some Test matches, some Test series even, do catch alight because, as in all good drama, the characters react to each other rather than look inwards at themselves. The difference today, compared with the 1960s, is that the public have something to compare Test cricket with, albeit only a one-day game. Whereas one kind of cricket-lover knows that wins and losses do not matter, provided the teams have gone into the game in the expectation of winning rather than with a determination not to lose, there is another cricket-lover, no less ardent, who expects and gets victory and defeat in his kind of cricket. While a draw can be a worthy result, giving honour to both sides, it is not an option available in the one-day game.

The danger with this, if we extend the philosophy of victory and defeat into a wider context, is that both players and spectators come to accept the fact that, as there must be a winner, there has to be a loser. Losing becomes as inevitable a part of the game as winning. That may be all right in play; in life it cannot be acceptable, and yet it has come to be accepted. If we entertain the Cardus precept that cricket holds the mirror up to English nature, what kind of Englishness is it that says there can be only winners and losers? Has cricket educated society to the fact that there is no longer an alternative, and hardened people's hearts against the losers? When purgatory no longer lies between heaven and hell, society is left with Churchill's warning to the House of Commons in 1940. 'Victory at all costs . . . for without victory there is no survival.' In the society of win or lose, there are those for whom survival is no longer a matter of the struggle for an honourably drawn life but a matter of time until the inevitable defeat.

The newspapers – some of them, anyway – pursue a policy of regarding defeat as failure; or could it be that the policy has followed the newspapers? Yet it was not only the press and the public that developed this perception of defeat as failure. The game did as well. When in the autumn of 1984 the Test and County Cricket Board commissioned an enquiry, under the chairmanship of its former chairman, Charles Palmer, it was against the background of 'widespread disappointment and genuine concern about the standards of play at Test and county level following a series of failures at international level . . .' Not defeats or losses, but failures.

Unlike Mr Murray's Structure Working Party of 1991–92, whose eight members, with the exception of the Somerset captain, Chris Tavaré, numbered just eleven first-class games between them, eight of the nine members of the Palmer enquiry had played Test cricket. This showed in their sensible and detailed analysis of the state of English cricket at the time. And it was reflected in the way their report – while bearing in mind 'the many and various, and in some cases essential benefits to cricket at all levels that accrue from a successful England team upholding the highest standards of the game in all respects both on and off the field' – first and foremost concerned itself with standards of play.

Although the counties initially rejected the planks of the Palmer Report, a number of its recommendations were subsequently taken on board. Not least among these were an organized structure for the development of potential excellence in young cricketers, and the greater use of facilities at the National Recreation Centre at Lilleshall. Considering standards at international level, the enquiry recommended that one of the England selectors should be appointed to a *full-time* position 'to act in conjunction with the Panel of Selectors and possibly act as Assistant Manager for overseas tours'. In the summer of 1986, partly in response to the Palmer Report and partly in response to the poor impression made by Gower's side in the West Indies the previous spring, the TCCB announced that it would be drawing up Terms of Reference for the position of assistant-manager on England tours, giving emphasis to players' fitness, practice facilities and day-to-day discipline. The role, it was revealed, would be reviewed at the spring meeting in 1987, with a view to the appointment continuing during the English season, possibly with a change of title. However, the Board did stress the feeling among its members that one man should not have full control of the England team. At the same time, it was announced that Micky Stewart would be assistant-manager of the side that Mike Gatting would captain in Australia that winter.

The men responsible for English cricket had never been comfortable with the prospect of one man having control of the England team. While divide and rule was never a deliberate policy, select and sack was a suitable substitute. For much of the 1960s, in particular, England players came and went with such frequency that it was never possible for any one person, as captain, to engender the kind of team spirit that would give him a natural authority. Hutton enjoyed this in the 1950s, as did May after him; each had his own team; each did things his own way. 'Peter had a knack of being able to ignore completely something he didn't want to bother with,' said Cowdrey, his vice-captain in Australia and the West Indies. Such independence, however, was anathema to some England selectors, who had their own opinions on how the game should be played. When Walter Robins became chairman of selectors in 1962, the new Selection Committee decided that one of their number would act as manager of the England team at each of the forthcoming Test matches against Pakistan. And it was only a year after Mike Smith had taken his side unbeaten through South Africa in 1964–65, building up and benefiting from a strong team spirit, that MCC imposed on him a tour manager for Australia who would ensure that the game was played according to the selectors' vision rather than the players' intentions.

The thought that there should be a full-time England 'team manager' crossed few people's minds. If it did, it was written off as a concept belonging to soccer, a professional game in which the captain was no more than a foreman. The manager was ... well, he was the boss. Wasn't Spurs captain Danny Blanchflower dropped from the side because he had the temerity (or the initiative) to move two players to different positions during a match? In cricket, if the captain wasn't exactly the boss, he was at least, in the eyes of the selectors, running his own shoot. Together the selectors and captain chose the side, and it was assumed that the players they picked were the best available and would give of their best for their country. Where was the need for a team manager?

In the West Indies, in 1964–65, an answer was put forward. Bobby Simpson's Australians were playing Garry Sobers' men for what was billed as cricket's world-title bout, and at the end of the series, which was won two Tests to one by West Indies, Sobers made particular mention of the role Sir Frank Worrell had played as manager. He was also the first to admit how fortunate he had been, in his first series as captain, to be leading a side that had built up such a wonderful team spirit in the years of Worrell's captaincy.

Appointing a manager for the series had been a departure for the West Indies Board, whose policy in the past had been to appoint a different manager for each island. But as E. W. Swanton pointed out when presciently suggesting the appointment of Worrell several months earlier, 'There are unusual problems about looking after a West Indian side at home. No first-class cricket is played (other than that by the touring team) to keep everyone fit and match-hard. The best practice and strict team discipline between Tests is therefore crucial . . . There is also the consideration of the tactical influence that Worrell could bring to bear if he saw the series through.'* Such considerations would not have been regarded as applying to English cricket, where the tradition of the captain as an amateur and a gentleman, and if possible an Oxbridge Blue, still had many influential supporters. In practice, however, a good case could be made for a 'supremo' to bring together the disparate talents of county cricket and weld them into a Test team. One or two counties had employed a manager to support their captain – Kent with Leslie Ames and Lancashire with Cyril Washbrook were examples – but it would be twenty

* *The Cricketer*, 6 November 1964

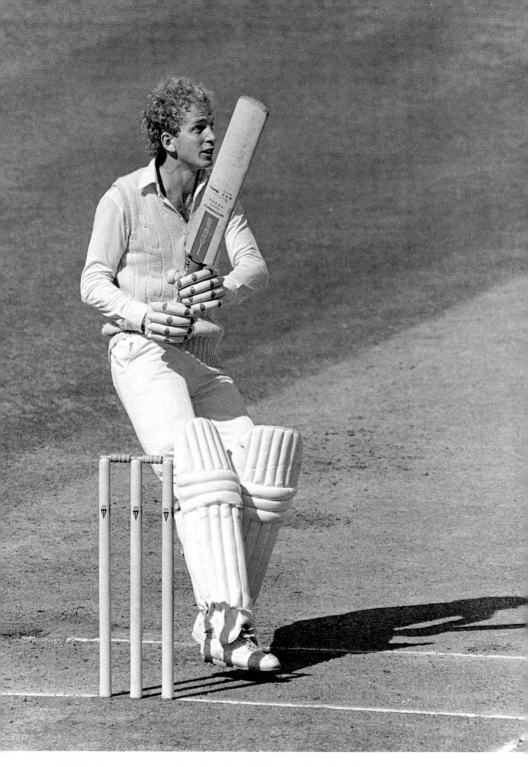

Golden Gower: at times he played on a different plane from his peers; there were moments when it looked as if he was living there as well.

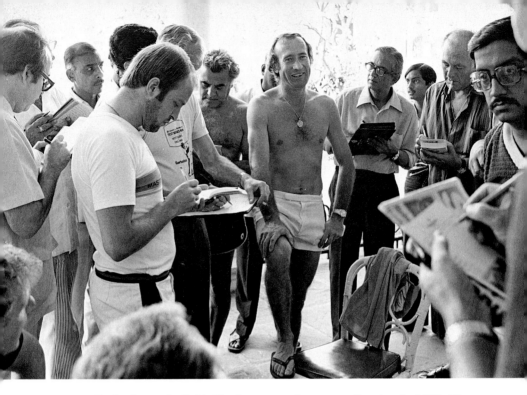

England captain Keith Fletcher meets the press at Bombay in 1981–82. Eleven years on, when the Essex guru was team manager, concern was voiced over the England players' dress in India.

Less happy days: Peter Lush, Mike Gatting and Micky Stewart face criticism of England's on-field behaviour at Christchurch in 1987–88.

The balcony scene from Headingley, 1989. Ted Dexter *(right)* was looking towards Alan Knott but looked to David Gower to set the tone and style for the England team. Australia, meanwhile, were setting the pace.

Graham Gooch and Micky Stewart put less emphasis on tone and style and more on commitment. They won more games than friends.

Reading the riot act: Imran Khan gives Salim Yousuf a piece of his mind for
claiming to catch Ian Botham 'on the hop' at Headingley in 1987.

Sultan of swing: as the innings progressed Waqar Younis had a ball and
batsmen the world over found themselves in dire straits.

Ken Barrington *(left)* and John Edrich put the Kiwis to flight at Headingley in 1965 with their second-wicket partnership of 369.

Not so much a run-out as a knock-out. Geoff Boycott's rush of blood ruined Derek Randall's hero's return to Trent Bridge in 1977.

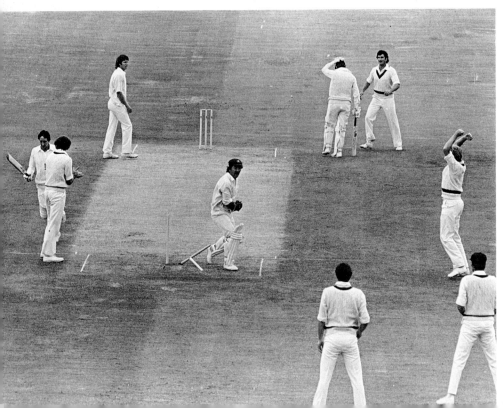

Another brick in the wall. 'We have lived to see and extol an honest artisan such as Boycott building his brick wall of an innings,' wrote Neville Cardus in 1964. A decade later, the Yorkshireman was a master builder.

National hero: Ian Botham's match-winning performances against Australia in 1981 put a spring in the step of all Englishmen and women.

years or more before the counties together were prepared to accept that the need existed for a full-time England team manager.

Their reluctance was understandable. For one thing, such an appointment entailed recognizing that the county game was no longer able to produce enough good players to go straight from county cricket into Test cricket. Australia, West Indies and South Africa brought this home during the sixties, but regular defeats of India, New Zealand and Pakistan helped everyone to forget what was painfully obvious. It took the improvement of the last-mentioned three as Test-match countries to make English cricket face up to the fact that hubris was a recipe for humiliation. But accepting that there might be a need for a team manager raised the question of finding someone suitable: someone whom they, the counties, could keep under their control. The prospect of a 'supremo' manager, along the same lines as the England football manager, was no more digestible to them than a 'supremo' captain had been in the days of Hutton and May. If they had to have anyone at all, they wanted an employee, and their decision in 1987 to appoint Micky Stewart for three years – as a way of building on the success achieved in Australia during the winter and of achieving continuity – fell right in line with Brook's Law. 'There are two reasons for making an appointment,' said Lord Norman-brook, a former head of the Civil Service. 'Either there was nobody else, or there *was* somebody else.'

In this instance there was somebody else. Several somebodies, in fact, and the man hotly tipped outside the TCCB boardroom was the former England captain, Ray Illingworth, 'technically the best of the post-war captains – and a great one at Test level' in the opinion of Wilf Wooller, the great man of Glamorgan cricket and an England selector from 1955 to 1961. It might not have been an opinion that endeared Illingworth to all members of the Test and County Cricket Board, for this was a case of like recognizing like. Wooller was his own man, a hard man, and he bowed to no one. Nor did Illingworth.

Ray Illingworth came to captaincy late in his career, being well into his thirty-seventh year when he joined Leicestershire as captain in 1969 after a contractual difference with Yorkshire. It was a shrewd signing by Leicestershire, for as an off-spinning all-rounder Illingworth had few peers in England. The previous summer he had played in three of the Tests against Australia, giving England an outside chance of victory at Headingley when he took six for 87 in fifty-one overs in Australia's second innings, but there was nothing to suggest he would add significantly to his tally of twenty-nine caps won over the past ten years. As it happened, he more than doubled it in the next five years as England's captain, during which time they regained the Ashes in Australia, retained them at home, and also won series against New Zealand, Pakistan and West Indies.

The captaincy of England came to him through a series of other men's misfortunes. His immediate predecessor, Colin Cowdrey, snapped the Achilles tendon in his left leg in May 1969 and Illingworth, within two months of taking over at Grace Road, was appointed in his place. Yet Cowdrey himself had regained the captaincy only because a jury of elders made untenable Brian Close's appointment to lead the MCC side to the West Indies in 1967–68. Close, Illingworth's captain at Yorkshire, had come to the job in 1966 at Cowdrey's expense, while Cowdrey had replaced M. J. K. Smith after England had lost the First Test against West Indies that summer by an innings with two days remaining. This defeat, at Old Trafford, was England's first in three days since Bradman's 1938 Australians beat them at Leeds. Against West Indies at Headingley in 1966, England survived for four days before going down by an innings in mid-afternoon, and Cowdrey, the captain, was one of six players to be dropped by the selectors for the Fifth and final Test.

Close, captaining his country for the first time, turned the tables on the West Indians at The Oval, and England's victory by an innings and 34 runs went a long way to assuaging the humiliations of the summer. Everything he did was positive, or so it seemed, and everything positive was rewarded with success. Some critics were apprehensive of Close's tough attitude, and tragically Robertson-Glasgow was no longer there to remind them that this was a Test match. In the field, Close set a splendid example, positioning himself in close-to-the-bat positions and using his bowlers shrewdly; despite the intense heat – from Thursday to Saturday the capacity crowd had to cope with a heatwave as well as the drama of England's fluctuating fortunes – the England players responded to him.

After the previous Test the selectors had discarded their best fast bowler, John Snow, only to recall him at the last minute when Price, his replacement, was injured. And under Close's style of captaincy Snow excelled, not just with the ball but also with the bat. The West Indians, already frustrated by England's recovery from a parlous 166 for seven by an eighth-wicket partnership of 217 between Graveney and John Murray, were then kept in the field for two more hours by Ken Higgs and Snow, England's last-wicket pair. Treating spin from the old ball and pace from the new with equal composure, these two put on 128 in a diverting stand which took them to within two runs of the Test record for the tenth wicket, set at Sydney in 1903–04 by R. E. Foster and Wilfred Rhodes against Australia. Neither Higgs nor Snow had hit a half-century in first-class cricket before – they finished with 63 and 59 not out respectively – while Murray's 112 was more than double his previous best Test score. Never before had the last three batsmen in the order scored a hundred and two half-centuries, and when West Indies batted again, Snow and wicket-keeper Murray combined to send back both openers with just 12 runs on the board. In addition they sent every Englishman at the ground that day home in a joyous mood.

Snow's first over on Monday morning sealed West Indies' fate. First Illingworth ran out David Holford, Sobers' cousin, with a pin-point throw from third man; next ball Snow, following Close's instructions, bounced the incoming Sobers, whose attempted hook went no further than his own box, whence it rebounded to the predatory Close at short leg. In West Indies' first innings, Sobers had been a victim of Close's adventurous captaincy when he pulled a long-hop from Barber to Graveney's safe hands. As with the second-innings dismissal of the West Indian captain there was much good fortune involved; none the less Close had introduced Barber's leg-spin into his attack early in the game, and he did persevere with it. Barber's five wickets in the match rewarded his enterprise. When, just after lunch on the fourth day, Barber caught and bowled Lance Gibbs to wrap up the innings and the match, all of England acclaimed a great triumph, and there were some who wondered if the right Yorkshireman was leading England from Downing Street. A letter to *The Times* suggested that England's victory at The Oval 'might prove a guide to the future conduct of Britain's affairs to Government, industry and trades unions alike'.

When India were comprehensively beaten in all three Tests in 1967, and England were one-up against Pakistan with one Test to play later that season, there seemed no reason why Close would not take the MCC side to the Caribbean in the winter. However, in the week before the Third Test Close, captaining Yorkshire in pursuit of a second successive Championship title, was accused of delaying tactics in a match at Edgbaston. Warwickshire, having bowled out the county champions twice, needed to score 142 runs for victory in 102 minutes, but in that time Yorkshire bowled only twenty-four overs, a rate of less than fifteen an hour when the accepted rate was twenty. In the last half-hour only six overs were bowled, and even allowing for a stoppage because of rain, the last two overs, bowled by Trueman and Richard Hutton, occupied eleven minutes. As a result of this time-wasting, adhered to despite the exhortations of umpire Elliott, Warwickshire fell nine runs short of their target and Yorkshire gained two undeserved points for achieving a draw.

Although Warwickshire lodged no complaint about Close's tactics, they were the subject of wide coverage in the press, and because waste of time constituted unfair play, the matter was presumably reported to Lord's by Messrs Elliott and Gray, the umpires, in accordance with the First-Class Regulations. The upshot was that a committee of former county captains, under the chairmanship of A. E. R. Gilligan of Sussex, the president-designate of MCC, was set up to report on the incident. It met on 23 August, the day before the start of The Oval Test against Pakistan, and its findings damned Close's prospects of being named, at the end of that match, as captain of the side for the West Indies. By unanimous accord the committee decided that the tactics used by Yorkshire 'constituted unfair play and were against the best interests of the game . . . the committee held the captain, Brian Close, entirely responsible for these tactics. They have therefore severely censured him and this decision will be conveyed to the Yorkshire County Cricket Club.'

Close himself was quoted in the press as saying he had 'no recriminations or apologies to make. My conscience is clear. Yorkshire had no chance of winning and my job was to prevent the other side from winning. I did nothing that others have not done before in similar circumstances.' Nevertheless, Sir Neville Cardus put his finger on the nub of the problem when, setting aside for the moment the moral rights and wrongs of Close's action, he said it was 'poor-spirited because it offered the opposition no chance to answer back'. A batsman couldn't score, 'can't even cheat!' exclaimed Cardus, if he didn't receive sufficient bowling in a given time. The counties took the point, and from the following season a minimum of twenty overs had to be bowled from the commencement of the last hour of a match.

It was suggested at the time that Close lost the England captaincy not so much because of the actual incident, but because implicit in his refusal to apologize was the proposition that he did not regard his action as unfair play. Jack Bailey, who had recently joined MCC as an additional assistant-secretary, remembered those turbulent days of August 1967 in a different light.

The fact that he did not apologize is quoted against Close, the impression being given that this was almost as big a crime as the time-wasting itself. I just do not think he could have saved himself. The moving finger, having writ, was already moving on, pointing a return to the more familiar school of England captaincy: the less successful, cleverly self-effacing, supremely diplomatic one epitomized by Colin Cowdrey. The Committee were determined to uphold the principle of fair play on the field and to be seen to be doing it; and in their eyes the removal of Close was the inevitable outcome.*

* Jack Bailey. *Conflicts in Cricket* (The Kingswood Press, 1989)

Close himself revealed in his autobiography that

Probably the whole secret lay in something I had been told a
month before, by a newspaperman, and it may perhaps indicate
the sort of influence these chaps can have when you know the
sort of 'information' they acquire. He said to me, 'For God's
sake, Brian, keep your nose clean because they are just waiting
at Lord's for a chance to prevent you leading the side in the
West Indies.'*

Certainly no English cricketer, let alone the England captain,
had been on the receiving end of such an official rebuke in modern
times. But they were changing times, as Close had every reason
to muse on when, in 1971, cricket's new governing body, the
Cricket Council, officially condemned certain incidents that had
occurred during the MCC tour of Australia in 1970–71. The
Cricket Council had been set up in 1968 and comprised representatives of MCC and two newly formed bodies, the Test and County
Cricket Board and the National Cricket Association.

The Cricket Council have considered the report of the committee set up to review all aspects of the 1970/71 Australasian
Tour. The Council are unanimous in expressing their pleasure
at the success of the team in winning both series of Test Matches.
However, the Cricket Council, as the Governing Body of Cricket
in the United Kingdom, must record their grave concern about
incidents involving dissent from umpires' decisions whether by
word or deed. Whilst appreciating the strains and stresses under
which cricket at the highest level is played, the Council must
warn all players that such conduct, which is contrary to the
spirit and tradition of the game and brings it into disrepute, will
not be tolerated.
    In dealing with such breaches of discipline, the Council and
the Test and County Cricket Board, through their Disciplinary
Committee, will not hesitate to use their wide powers which

* Brian Close. *I Don't Bruise Easily* (Macdonald and Jane's, 1978)

include the termination of the registration of a player. The Selection Committee have been instructed accordingly and copies of ˙ is statement have been sent to all County Clubs.

While being a strongly worded statement it did not, however, mention any player by name. Nor did it make any reference to the captain whose responsibility it had been to ensure on-field discipline. In the final Test, at Sydney, Illingworth had wagged his finger provocatively in umpire Rowan's face when Snow was warned for persistent use of the bouncer after an Australian tail-ender, Terry Jenner, had ducked into a short delivery. When the crowd then vented its anger on the England fast bowler as he took up his fielding position on the long-leg boundary, Illingworth led his men off the field without any obvious word to the umpires. Only when he was warned that England would forfeit the match did Illingworth take them back on the field.

After the Fifth Test at Melbourne, Illingworth had criticized Messrs O'Connell and Rowan, the umpires there, for unfairness in warning Snow for intimidation while allowing the Australian fast bowler, Alan 'Froggy' Thomson, much greater licence. 'Apart from the principle of a captain criticizing umpires both specifically and by implication,' wrote E. W. Swanton in his diary for *The Cricketer*, 'one's view on this particular outburst is that it was ill-timed, injudicious, undignified and unjustified. Some sort of Australian retaliation is almost certain to follow; nor can any good purpose be served.'

Sober words indeed, and soon he was needing more when, on the first day of the Sixth Test at Adelaide, Boycott on being adjudged run out by umpire O'Connell not only threw his bat away in a fit of pique but indulged in some abusive back-chat. 'A degree of displeasure' is how it was later described. Michael Melford relied on plainer language when reporting the day's play in the *Daily Telegraph*, calling Boycott's behaviour 'the worst exhibition of its kind' he had seen. In the *Adelaide Advertiser*, Barry Richards considered the reaction of young cricketers. 'They might think that if a great player can throw his bat away when he didn't agree with the umpire, then why can't I?' Poor

Mr Swanton merely recalled 'the courtesies of combat, which
the old professionals were as zealous in preserving as any
amateur'.

With the exception of the vice-captain, Cowdrey, who had an
unhappy fifth tour of Australia, Illingworth's men were the new
breed of professional cricketers, for whom the victory was as
important, if not more important, than the game. They played for
him as they would have played – had played, some of them – for
Brian Close, and no one on that tour pulled out the stops for his
captain more than John Snow. As often moody as mean, Snow
had a reputation for trying only when it pleased him. But Illingworth won Snow's respect because, as captain, he fought for his
players' rights and privileges. He was a team man. Snow repaid
him with a series of hostile performances which were instrumental
in England's returning with the Ashes.

Illingworth returned with more than the Ashes, though. He
came home with his reputation as a tactical captain enhanced. He
had no serious challenger for the position, and in omitting to name
any player in its condemnation of those incidents in Australia, the
Cricket Council was tacitly recognizing and accepting this. Would
the statement have been as conciliatory four years earlier when
cricket in England was governed by MCC? Probably not. Once
more the power rested with the players, and in Illingworth there
was again a 'supremo'. It took two heavy defeats by an old-
fashioned cricketer in Garry Sobers to unseat him. And when,
more than a decade later, there was a chance that Illingworth
would fill that role again, this time as England team manager, the
counties balked at the prospect.

>   At Viscount Nelson's lavish funeral,
>   While the mob milled and yelled about St Paul's,
>   A General chatted with an Admiral:
>
>   'One of your Colleagues, Sir, remarked today
>   That Nelson's *exit*, though to be lamented,
>   Falls not inopportunely, in its way.'

'He was a thorn in our flesh' came the reply . . .
                         . . .
'Yet,' cried the General, 'six-and-twenty sail
Captured or sunk by him off Tráfalgár –
That writes a handsome *finis* to the tale.'

'Handsome enough. The seas are England's now.
That fellow's foibles need no longer plague us.
He died most creditably, I'll allow.'

'And, Sir, the secret of his victories?'
'By his unServicelike, familiar ways, Sir,
He made the whole Fleet love him, damn his eyes!'*

* From *1805* by Robert Graves

10

The Price of Packer

'No captain of a touring team since D. R. Jardine nearly 40 years ago,' began E. M. Wellings, 'has had such a difficult task as Raymond Illingworth, leader of MCC in Australia in 1970–71.'* It was an apt comparison, for all that Illingworth was less the master of his own fate than Jardine had been. Both aroused the antagonism of the Australian crowds: Jardine because of what he represented, with his patrician disdain for them; Illingworth because he was too tough for an Australian sporting image that had begun to curl at the edges. In adversity both became the nucleus of the strong team spirit that carried their teams to victory. And inadvertently both were captains of MCC tours that demonstrated the importance that the game's administrators put on money.

Jack Fingleton put it succinctly, as always, in *Cricket Crisis*, his classic account of the bodyline series. 'When a principle of cricket was at stake in 1933, the Australian Board of Control, which had raised that principle, quickly dropped it when the MCC committee suggested cancelling the rest of the tour, including two Test matches.' Whereas in Adelaide, venue of the Third Test, the Australian Board saw fit to advise MCC that, 'In our opinion the tactics of your team are unsporting,' by Brisbane, before the Fourth Test almost a month later, they were telling Lord's, 'We do not regard the sportsmanship of your team as being in question.'

'What frightened the Board of Control more than bodyline in 1932–33,' Fingleton wrote, 'was the MCC suggestion that the

---

* *Wisden Cricketers' Almanack 1972*

rest of the tour, with its two remunerative Test matches, should be cancelled. No deadlier yorker had been bowled in any Test series.'

Illingworth's situation in 1970–71 was the reverse, in that MCC didn't threaten to end his tour; it added a Test match to it midway through the series. In one sense it wasn't an extra game, for the additional Test match replaced MCC's return fixture against Victoria, and a one-day game up country. Furthermore it was arranged because the scheduled Third Test, at Melbourne, had to be abandoned when near-continuous rain prevented a start. Almost universally the decision was hailed as imaginative and positive, and one cricket writer, Alan Ross, hoped that 1971 would 'go down as the year when the first steps were taken to do away with the inconclusiveness of Test cricket'. Less enthusiastic were the MCC players. Although not having to endure more cricket than they'd been selected for, they none the less felt that loading the tour with another Test match tipped the balance of the series in Australia's favour. In that, they did have a point.

Party to the rearranged schedule was the Australian Board of Control, represented by Sir Donald Bradman and Bob Parish, and the Cricket Council, whose chairman, Sir Cyril Hawker, and vice-chairman, Gubby Allen, happened to be in Melbourne – and happened also, by design rather than chance, to be president and treasurer respectively of MCC. Another in on the act was the tour manager, David Clark, who was on the MCC committee. All good men and true, but in doing what they thought best for cricket they were opening a Pandora's box.

As England teams, and those of other countries, have hurtled through tours playing Test matches with barely a pause – except for the plethora of one-day internationals – we have heard a constant appeal that there should be fewer Test matches; that their frequency has devalued them in the eyes of the cricket public. I have made the same protest, and I believe with good reason. But unlike some of the critics making that call, I was not among those who shouted 'Hooray' when the men good and true forced that extra Test match on Illingworth's touring team. In fact, one wonders whether some of those 'Hooray' Henrys should have been shouting in the first place. Many of them were, after all, Englishmen, and one would assume that they wanted England to regain the Ashes, even if Colin Cowdrey wasn't captain of the team. To whose benefit was a rescheduled tour that went Fourth Test, Sydney (January 9–14), a non-first-class match at Newcastle (January 16–18), Fifth Test, Melbourne (January 21–26), Sixth Test, Adelaide (January 29–February 3), three one-day games against assorted opposition (February 6, 8, 9) and Seventh Test, Sydney (February 12–17)? Surely it was more to Australia's. As host country they had a ready supply of players in the event of injuries. Illingworth could call only on those he had in his tour party, and with no first-class matches between the Tests, he had no opportunity to give his reserves the right kind of match practice to prepare them for Test cricket. Moreover, while the rearrangement brought Australia some £70,000 in gate money, English cricket, *Wisden* tells us, 'received no share of the extra revenue' for compromising the chances of its own team. Just whose side were Sir Cyril Hawker and G. O. Allen on?

The answer, an honest enough one, would be that they were on the side of cricket. That is how, as men of MCC, they played the game. National interests would not have entered their considerations; had they been in the Foreign Office they could not have acted out of finer motives. 'In spite of his travels,' Edmund Wilson said of Harold Nicolson, 'he has resided in one country – the British Foreign Office.' By substituting Marylebone Cricket Club for British Foreign Office, the same could be said of Gubby Allen. MCC was his country, cricket was its established religion and Lord's was its cathedral. In time, thinking first and foremost of cricket's interests, he would unconsciously betray MCC and be betrayed by cricket. The Foreign Office couldn't have done it better.

Before that happened, though, MCC and the Cricket Council found themselves let down by Australian cricket. The ball that set this particular betrayal in motion popped out of Pandora's box in front of some 46,000 people, although few if any at the Melbourne Cricket Ground that January day in 1971 could have known how far it would roll. The occasion was the first one-day 'Test' – the first limited-overs game between two full international sides from the Test-playing countries. It was played on what would have been the final day of the abandoned Third Test, and Australia won by five wickets, bowling England out for 190 in 39.4 overs and reaching their target in 34.6 overs. Each innings was limited to forty eight-ball overs, and some of the details show how touchingly innocent the Australians were about one-day cricket. An off-spinner, Ashley Mallett, and a leg-spinner, Keith Stackpole, took three wickets each for them – Illingworth also took three for England – while their batsmen hit a six and seventeen fours in contrast to the eight boundaries notched by the more tactical Englishmen. When they next met in this kind of cricket, in England in 1972 over 55 overs for the Prudential Trophy, England won the series by two matches to one.

The Prudential Assurance company, in addition to sponsoring every one-day international series played in England from 1972 to 1983, put up the money and the trophy for the first three World Cup tournaments, in 1975, 1979 and 1983. Given the endless number of one-day internationals played now, driving out the Test match 'as inexorably as the grey squirrel drove out the red',* it seems strange to note that only eighteen such games had been played world-wide prior to the 1975 World Cup. And of those eighteen, only one, other than the original fixture, was played by Australia in Australia, England winning by three wickets at Melbourne on New Year's Day, 1975.

In that it brought a win against Australia, that game offered Mike Denness's side a little solace halfway through a tour in which they were already two down in the Test series. It might have been three down, for the previous evening, at the end of a tense, low-scoring Third Test, Australia with eight wickets down had been eight runs from victory. However, they won the next two Tests, by 171 runs and 163 runs, and England's innings victory at Melbourne at the end of the tour was hardly even a consolation prize. Of much greater consolation to the beleaguered England

* John Woodcock. *Wisden Cricketers' Almanack 1985*

batsmen was the absence through injury of Australia's new fast bowler, Jeff Thomson.

Scarcely more than a spear carrier on his first Test appearance, against Pakistan in 1972–73, Thomson returned to the international stage two years later to hurl a sequence of thunderbolts at a succession of bewildered Englishmen. By the time he sprained his right shoulder, playing tennis on the rest day of the Fifth Test at Adelaide, he had taken thirty-three wickets and impressed himself deeply on the psyche of the touring team. He had also found a place in the heart of Australian crowds countrywide by dint of his ferocious assault on the old enemy. For all the concern that Thomson showed, it didn't matter much whether they were young or old; as long as they wore an England cap they were the enemy.

As if facing Thomson wasn't sufficiently daunting, England also had to contend with Dennis Lillee, who in England in 1972 had taken thirty-one wickets in the five Tests, a record for an Australian bowler in England. Through sheer speed and bounce he had unsettled all of England's specialist batsmen then, and on Australian soil, with the large crowds baying 'Lill . . . lee, Lill . . . lee' as he began his long, threateningly graceful run to the wicket, he unleashed a hostile attack on an ill-prepared England line-up. Ill prepared because Lillee's fitness, let alone his blazing speed, must have taken the tourists by surprise. A year and a half earlier, in the West Indies, his back had rebelled against the demands he was making on it, and there were fears in some quarters that he would not bowl again. It was why the England selectors – Alec Bedser, Jack Bond, Brian Taylor and Ossie Wheatley – had chosen their side for Australia on the assumption that their opponents were unlikely to have a genuinely fast bowler, let alone two. Where, one wonders, was their intelligence?

E. W. Swanton was right when he wrote in 1971, during ill-tempered times on MCC's previous tour of Australia, that 'Some sort of Australian retaliation is almost certain to follow; nor can any good purpose be served'. Australian retaliation was proving to be harsh and humiliating, and it was being dealt out by a cricketer every bit as hard as Ray Illingworth. Ian Chappell was not every Englishman's cup of tea, and that meant he was just the man for Australians. His grandfather, Vic Richardson, had captained Australia in South Africa in 1935–36, having been vice-captain to Woodfull in England in 1930, and the man who once hooked Harold Larwood into the pavilion at the Adelaide Oval had passed his courage and his skill on to his daughter's eldest son. Ian Chappell had played for South Australia at eighteen and for Australia when he was twenty-one, making his debut against Pakistan in 1964–65.

If the England selectors might be forgiven for underestimating the strength of Australia's fast bowling, they had no reason to underestimate the character of the man determined to wrest the Ashes from them. In 1972 Chappell brought to England a young side which was given odds of three to one against recovering the Ashes. They didn't manage to do that, but in the final Test, at The Oval, they did square the series. England had won at Old Trafford and Headingley, Australia had won at Lord's, where on his debut the Western Australian fast-medium swing bowler, Bob Massie, took sixteen wickets in the match. At the time only two bowlers, Jim Laker with nineteen wickets and Sydney Barnes with seventeen, had bettered this feat. An already dramatic series was intensified further when the Headingley Test finished in three days after the England left-arm spinner, Derek Underwood, took ten wickets in the match on a pitch which was without pace and took spin from the opening day. The weekend before, the Leeds ground had been flooded by a thunderstorm, and this prevented frequent use of the heavy roller in the days before the match. Bill Bowes, reporting the match for *Wisden*, said that the pitch was not up to Test match standard, but the Test and County Cricket Board's Pitches Committee exonerated the Yorkshire groundsman when it was established that fusarium disease had spread while the covers were on and had killed much of the grass before it could be treated. Still, 'Batting on both sides was flimsy,' according to Bowes, and the totals bore him out. Australia were dismissed for 146 and 136; England's first-innings reply would have been just as miserable had it not been for the eighth-wicket stand of 104 between Illingworth and Snow. The former played a truly gritty captain's innings, holding out for four and a half hours to make 57, the highest score of the match.

At The Oval, it took Ian Chappell and his younger brother, Greg, just over four hours to add 201 for Australia's third wicket, in which time Greg Chappell scored 113 runs in a stylish, upright manner which made a handsome contrast to his brother's pugnacious approach. It was his third hundred against England in ten Tests, his Test career having begun with 108 against them at Perth in 1970–71. Ian Chappell's 118 took five and a half hours, and provided the first instance of two brothers hitting a hundred in the same innings of a Test match. Nineteen months later the brothers went one better – or perhaps two better – by scoring hundreds in each innings of the Wellington Test against New Zealand.

Under Chappell's imaginative leadership, the Australians played positive, entertaining cricket in England in 1972, and did so again in the West Indies the following spring. West Indies were going through an uncertain period of transition, and by the time the Australians triumphed two–nil in the five-match series, the West Indians had gone twenty games since 1969 without a win. It was a sequence they brought to an end in England several months later, and it was in ending their unhappy run that they also brought to an end, at the age of forty-one, Illingworth's reign as captain of England. He was the only Test captain to have the measure of Ian Chappell. Had Illingworth been on the field on the last day at The Oval in 1972 – he had sprained his ankle while bowling the previous evening – Australia might have struggled to square the series, even though England were unable to call on Snow and Basil D'Oliveira because of injuries. Without a peer as a Test match tactician, he had given Chappell a fiery baptism and a well-heeded lesson in his first Test as Australia's captain: the controversy-filled final Test of the 1970–71 series which England won to be sure of the Ashes.

Just as Illingworth brought out the best in his players by gaining their respect and drawing on their professionalism, Ian Chappell moulded around his own aggressive personality a team that overflowed with confidence. Just as Illingworth's players responded to him because they trusted him to protect their interests, so Chappell's men gave him their all because he did not kowtow to conventions or establishments. If they sometimes looked more like desperados than cricketers, they were a happy band of outlaws. Equally important was the way they filled a need in Australia's sporting culture. The crowds poured into cricket grounds in their thousands in 1974–75 to watch their new heroes sort out Denness's poms. The first-day attendance of 77,165 at Melbourne for the Third Test was the third largest for a day's play at a Test match – Melbourne also having the largest and second-largest attendances – and the 178,027 who attended the Fourth Test set a record for the Sydney Cricket Ground. Just under 100,000 watched the Fifth Test at the Adelaide Oval, and even though Australia were four-nil up in the series more than 100,000 went to the Melbourne Cricket Ground when Australia and England returned there for the Sixth Test. When Clive Lloyd's West Indians toured Australia in 1975–76, expectations were high that, with the series even, 100,000 would pack into the MCG on the opening day of the Third Test. Australia had won at Brisbane and the West Indians had drawn level at Perth. However, Boxing Day on the beach still held its traditional appeal and the authorities had to settle for a crowd of 85,596, more than the total attendance at any of the Test match grounds except Lord's during the Australians' tour of England in 1975. It exceeded the attendance Australia and England had drawn the previous year in Melbourne and it provided evidence, were evidence needed, that Australian cricket was now 'big bucks'.

One man was particularly aware of this, and he was perfectly placed to take advantage of the dissatisfaction that was festering between the players and the Australian cricket establishment. He had wealth, he had his own television channel, he was accustomed to getting his way, and he was in dispute with the Australian Cricket Board. What he wanted was the exclusive television rights for Australian cricket, and these the Australian Board was not prepared to concede. It already had obligations to the Australian Broadcasting Commission, which it was not prepared to break, and its policy was not to give exclusive rights to any one Australian television channel.

Kerry Packer's interest in cricket had been whetted by the final of the first World Cup, in June 1975. Played on what, appropriately enough, was the longest day of the year, this 60-overs-a-side game began at eleven o'clock and finished seventeen minutes before nine o'clock – the same number of minutes as the number of runs by which Australia fell short of West Indies' 291 for eight. The longest day in cricket history, it engrossed not only the 26,000 who packed into Lord's but also the millions around the world who watched the game on television. The potential of such an audience for cricket was not lost on Packer. Cricket, he realized, was no longer simply a sporting occasion; it was a business opportunity. This was something the authorities in England had known for some years, but whereas for them the business was cricket, for Packer the business was commercial television.

When his approaches to the Australian Board were rebuffed, Packer reacted by buying up a number of international cricketers to contest a 'world series' of matches during the Australian season. Negotiations to sign players were conducted without a whisper reaching the ears of the authorities in Australia or England, demonstrating how any vessel can be watertight when lined with the right kind of paper. But when the story broke, and it became known that the leading protagonists among the players were the current England captain, Tony Greig, and the immediate past captain of Australia, Ian Chappell, the feeling of outrage within the cricket establishment knew no bounds. Packer, it was generally agreed, was little more than a pirate who had stepped outside the bounds of ordinary decency. All that could be said in Greig's defence was that he was an Englishman only by adoption – which was pretty obvious from the hungry, adventurous way he played his cricket.

Packer's essay into the comfortable world of cricket was a watershed. Both on the field and off it, cricket would never be the same again. Prior to Packer, Jack Bailey ventured in his book, *Conflicts in Cricket*,

We [cricket's administrators] had spent years nurturing the game from top to bottom, had found a broad basis of agreement about how it should be administered (though we had problems in always agreeing). At every level it was on an upward curve through the joint efforts of players and administrators. Traditional aspects of the game had always been to the forefront. Preserving the best of the old, even in the mini-revolution of one-day cricket that had taken place, had seemed of vital importance. Not only did Packer appear to be threatening these traditions, but he was a threat (let's be honest) to the self-esteem of those representing established cricket, and not simply because he had fallen out with our friends and allies the Australian Cricket Board.

Cricket's establishment had found itself to some degree in the same predicament that confronted national governments as they came to terms with the influence of multi-national corporations. Seeing that for the first time it no longer had full control of its own destiny, it sought means of clawing back its power.

Jack Bailey was at the time secretary of MCC, and consequently secretary of the International Cricket Conference, as it was then. For him, 'Cricket was one of the constant bastions of the ideals we hoped the world would one day live by'; its integrity should have been beyond question. Yet, in his words, 'Recognized cricket had been sold down the river by a number of players.'*

But had it? In England it had not been the players who turned cricket into a full-time occupation; it had been the counties. By restructuring county cricket so that all cricketers became professional sportsmen, and leaving no opening for the part-time cricketer, they had made all the players employees; and like employees in any occupation they were open to offers from another employer. All Packer had done, in his businesslike way, was a spot of headhunting. He wasn't asking anyone to break his contract, because none of the cricketers contracted to English

* Jack Bailey. *Conflicts in Cricket*

counties was under contract for the months when Packer wanted
them in Australia for his World Series Cricket tournaments. They
were free agents. Morally, it could be argued, they had obligations
to the established game – as did the Australians, for example –
but they had none under the law of the land, or under the Laws
of Cricket.

To cricket's cost, and in particular to English cricket's cost, the
matter went to the lawyers, and then to the courts, where Mr
Justice Slade declared that any changes to the rules of the ICC –
intended to prevent Packer's men from playing Test cricket – and
to the TCCB's conditions governing the qualification and registration of county cricketers were unreasonable restraints of trade.
The ruling should not have come as a surprise to the authorities,
for it was just as Trevor Bailey had forecast,* and his legal prac-
tices had ended when he left the Royal Marines. Still, as Bernard
Levin wrote in the course of detailing an interesting affair involving a young lady of favourable graces and a minister of state, 'One
of the more interesting things to emerge from this case, though
perhaps not widely enough, is the extraordinary naïvety of the
legal profession, and the even more extraordinary naïvety of other
people *towards* that profession.'†

The upshot, in the cricket case, was that the ICC and the TCCB
were landed with the costs, which amounted to the best part of a
quarter of a million pounds. It was something English cricket could
have done without, for all that the TCCB's finances had benefited
from Cornhill Insurance's sponsorship of Test cricket – and even
from Mr Packer, to whose Channel 9 they sold the Australian
television rights for the 1977 Ashes series between England and
Australia. In addition to the financial consequences to the game's
welfare, Packer's intrusion threatened friendships on and off the
field, and it exposed the parochialism of English cricket. While
some counties felt the Packer players should be kept out of county
cricket as well as Test cricket – the England selectors did not
choose any Packer men – others saw their non-selection by Eng-

---

* In a conversation with the author
† Bernard Levin. *The Pendulum Years: Britain and the Sixties*

land as enhancing their prospects in the domestic competitions. Among the casualties was the MCC president and ICC chairman, David Clark, who felt he could not remain on the committee of Kent, who had embraced their Packer players, while he was acting on behalf of the ICC against the Packer operation.

But the rub was yet to come. There had always been those who said that Packer's demand for television rights was an Australian problem; that it should not have involved English cricket. But by recruiting players who would otherwise have been eligible to tour overseas with England teams, and by signing virtually the whole West Indian Test team, Packer effectively made the issue an international one, and it was to the ICC that world cricket looked to effect a solution. An added complication was the impending World Cup, scheduled to be staged in England in June 1979. The refusal by cricketers in some countries to play against Packer players would be an unwelcome embarrassment at cricket's showpiece, for it was known that Pakistan and West Indies would select Packer players for the tournament. It was also known that some English players might refuse to play against them. Early in April that year, however, hints of a rapprochement came from John Arlott when he addressed the Cricketers' Association, of which he was president. 'We have been asked not to rock the boat,' he told England's first-class cricketers. 'We have been given assurances, but not facts, that close negotiations are going on between the two sides and that a settlement is hoped for in weeks rather than months.'*

He had been well informed. Towards the end of the month it was announced that the Australian Board had granted Packer's Channel 9 the exclusive rights for Test cricket and other matches in Australia, as a result of which World Series Cricket would be disbanded. Packer had what he wanted, though no quicker than if he had waited until the Australian Board's contract with the Australian Broadcasting Commission expired in 1979. Within a month, however, it transpired that Packer had obtained more than he initially bargained for: he and the Australian Board had signed

* Wisden Cricketers' Almanack 1980

a Nonaggression Pact which lacked only a Low cartoon. For two difficult years the world of cricket had stood alongside the Australian cricket authorities in their struggle against World Series Cricket, absorbing costs it could ill afford and keeping in place fragile links. Now Australian cricket had chosen to stand on its head, and it cared not who saw the colour of its underwear. As this would not always be white, it could be taken for granted that Australian cricket had forsaken any pretensions of purity. Its marriage to Packer may not have been a love match, but it went into the union with its legs wide open.

Among the offspring of this marriage of convenience is the remorseless programme of one-day cricket that swamps every Australian season and which requires the co-operation, always given, of two other Test-playing countries. England and West Indies were invited to attend the christening in 1979–80 – an offer neither could refuse – and ironically upstaged the parents by eliminating Australia from the World Series Cup finals. In a repeat of the 1979 World Cup final, West Indies came out on top in the best-of-three final series.

Each country also played three Test matches against Australia, after which the Test and County Cricket Board told the Australians that they wanted their next tour, in 1982–83, to revert to the traditional format of five or six Test matches. 'The Australian Board,' said a TCCB spokesman, 'have agreed to a significant reduction in one-day international cricket from their original programme. England are strongly of the opinion that there are still too many of these matches as opposed to Tests than is desirable.' All of which might have been taken with a pinch of snuff at Lord's, but was taken with a pinch of salt in Australia. England played ten one-day games in 1982–83, exactly the same number scheduled in 1979–80. Moreover, with the last five and a half weeks of their tour given over to one-day games, the Test programme of five matches had to be completed by the first week of January 1983. England lost the Ashes, going down by two Tests to one, and failed to reach the finals of the one-day series, which was contested by Australia and New Zealand. Had England played in the finals, they would have ended up playing more one-day games than in 1979–80! Still, the tour was a financial success, so everyone was happy.

The Australian Board, as part of its marriage settlement, also had to adopt the illegitimate twins of Packer cricket: day/night games and coloured clothing. The two were inseparable and created quite a spectacle, often with a rowdy crowd in attendance. A gladiatorial image of cricket had been promoted as an attraction of the Packer package, and it became a feature of Australian cricket. But while the aggressive marketing of cricket brought greater numbers to the game, those numbers were swelled by a loutish element whose drunken behaviour gave the cricket authorities headaches as well as themselves. The campaign of abuse to which Mike Brearley was subjected on England's tour in 1979–80 reached such a disgusting pitch that the Australian team manager felt obliged to issue a statement in which he said that the behaviour and language of some sections of the crowd had made him ashamed to be an Australian. In the early day/night games at Sydney, the England players found themselves the target of missiles as well as abuse, and the atmosphere some nights was more in keeping with Roman games at the Colosseum than a game of cricket.

Prior to the tour, the Test and County Cricket Board had stipulated that England would not play in coloured clothing or 'suffer any other intolerable gimmicks of WSC television presentation'. When the team arrived in Australia, however, Brearley, the captain, was put under pressure to accept those conditions which the TCCB had already rejected – coloured stripes on their clothing, the use of a white ball in daytime games as well as day/night games, and the thirty-yard restrictive fielding circles that had been introduced in World Series Cricket one-day games. He refused, but as the spokesman outlining England's objections to conditions which seemed designed principally for television, 'Brearley was portrayed as a "whingeing Pom", which was grossly unfair. It must be hoped that no future captain is ever landed with such a burden.'*

* *Wisden Cricketers' Almanack 1981*

Bob Willis wasn't. By the time he captained England in Australia in 1982–83, the Test and County Cricket Board had not only gone along with the Australian Board's 'If it's Monday it must be Melbourne' itinerary, but the players were into coloured clothing, albeit considerably less snazzy than the panelled outfits favoured by Australia and New Zealand. Ten years on, the same conditions had become part and parcel of English cricket. All that remained to be seen was if the Test and County Cricket Board, in taking on board one of Packer's twins, was unwittingly extending a welcome to the uncouth friends it had attracted in Australia.

I say unwittingly, when the temptation might have been to write irresponsibly, because policymakers so often deceive themselves that their world of meetings and manoeuvrings is the real one. It is not. The real world acts according to nature, not according to plan, which is why it catches the planners unaware and unprepared. English cricket always expresses surprise, indignation even, when one-day internationals are accompanied not only by the clamour of the immigrant supporters of touring teams but occasionally by sporadic outbursts of violence. Yet these are the condiments of cricket in their native lands, for all that England is technically their native land. Intentionally or unintentionally, like it or not, since Packer got his hands on the one-day international it has become the vehicle for nationalism in cricket. There is no more satisfaction in watching collared-and-tied Englishmen in hospitality boxes pouring lager and abuse on Indian supporters at The Oval than there is in having to listen to the constant taunting of opposing England and Pakistan supporters at Edgbaston. Racism is just as much a fact of English life as parochialism, and there is nothing new in that. C. T. 'Tris' Bennett, captain of Harrow in 1921 and of Cambridge University in 1925, recollected his experience of it in an article for the 1974 edition of *Wisden*.

Many people are under the impression that apartheid is a comparatively recent cult. This is not so. I am assured that his colour limited Ranjitsinhji's appearances in the 'Varsity match to one, in 1893. That is probably why 'Ranji' played so much of his cricket on Parker's Piece for sides with no University connection . . .

In my own time, I recall vividly the occasion when my team, playing on tour, received an invitation to attend the 21st birthday party of the daughter of a local civic dignitary. The invitation stated explicitly that the function was 'for whites only' – clearly an indication that Duleep would not be welcome. It was declined without thanks. The verbal reply of the late A. W. Carr, a member of the opposing team, was an astounding piece of unprintable oratory.

For the welfare of English cricket it is essential financially that India and Pakistan continue to attract large numbers of supporters from their immigrant populations. Without them, the attendances at Test matches, and even at one-day internationals, would be disappointing to the authorities. Fervent national support is in the TCCB's interest.

Parochial support of the counties is also in its interest, and one hopes that the Board is aware of what it is encouraging by emphasizing county identification through coloured clothing in the Sunday competition. I fear it has not looked beyond the commercial gains and has not taken account of the potential social ramifications. This is, after all, the organization that told the marketing manager of Gillette Industries that his company could give away razor products at a Gillette Cup final! Cricketers, wearing white, have long presented a neutral focus, even during the years when crowd behaviour at games suffered from intemperate imbibition – often of a sponsor's brew. Now the TCCB has decided not only to kit out the teams in identifiable colours but their supporters as well, if they want to buy team shirts in the manner of football fans. Football has shown that the Englishman has not forgotten his tribal ties, and it has cost football dear in controlling him. Cricket does not have that sort of money, and the TCCB has even less public goodwill than money. Bright young men at the Board, and some not so young or bright, hope that coloured clothing will attract a new spectator to the game. It will. It did in Australia, and where Australia leads, English cricket follows. What should be remembered is that not all the stock that made Australia what it is was exported. Some of it remained in England, and its descendants may find that the bright new cricket is just up their street some sunny summer Sunday.

11

Lost at Lord's

Viewing administrative decisions from a distance, even if that distance is no more than the remove from the Pavilion at Lord's to the Grace Gates, it is always disturbing when something gives the observer grounds to wonder about the degree of intelligence or sensitivity employed by the decision-makers. MCC did some daft things in their time, and dropped enough bricks to build the new Mound Stand without the German steel which increased in price as the German mark strengthened against the pound. One would have thought that the MCC committee, with its brigade of bankers and brokers, might have allowed for such a contingency but it appears not to have. The increased price paid for the steel was one of the reasons given when members were advised of a revised estimate of costs. Perhaps Lord Deedes' comment about the Cabinet Room at No. 10 Downing Street, apropos of the Long Room at Lord's, applies just as much these days to the Treasury.

Dropping bricks is one thing, but not even MCC revealed a propensity for shooting itself in the foot as sublimely as the Test and County Cricket Board has. The fact that members of one organization are often members of the other, of course, makes it less surprising that cricket in recent years has given the impression of hobbling from one crisis to another. A chiropodist could find full-time employment at Lord's, and have a company car thrown in to boot.

Decision-making, as opposed to policy-making, is a problem for all organizations governed ultimately by committee, as both MCC and the TCCB are. Committees, like cabinets, have a great advantage over individual management in that they provide an escape from personal responsibility and identity; but in any organization such as the TCCB there is a frequent need for a decision, and its full committee meets only three or four times a year. There is an Executive Committee, containing the chairmen of the different sub-committees, and there is a secretariat which administers, advises and fields the brickbats levelled at the Board by the press and the public. But it takes a confident, skilful administrator to make the off-the-cuff decisions that one day have to be justified to committees. There are enough examples of officials being left high and dry by their committees to persuade all but the bravest administrators to favour reaction ahead of action.

An incident in point was the TCCB's decision not to refund spectators when only two balls could be bowled on the second day of the 1992 Edgbaston Test between England and Pakistan. On the previous day the weather conditions had prevented a single ball being bowled, as a result of which spectators were entitled to their money back, and the thought lingered long in many minds that it had been in the Board's interest to get in those two balls of play on the second day to avoid incurring a similar refund. The opening day's abandonment had cost it around £150,000; estimates put the potential loss had there been no play on the second day in the region of a further quarter of a million pounds. The terms of the Board's insurance cover for refunds, in the event of play being washed out for the day, were based on loss spread over the season, as opposed to a daily loss. However, the two balls bowled by Phillip DeFreitas to the Pakistani opening batsmen gave the Board the opportunity to jump out of the frying pan into the fire, and it leapt at the opportunity. As Martin Johnson put it next morning in the *Independent*, the TCCB's gesture in offering free entry to second-day ticketholders on the final day of the match was tantamount to a finger for each ball bowled.

The weather has always been a hazard for cricketers, and for no one more than the paying spectator. Play was never guaranteed, and for generations the game's fans waited patiently, watching the umpires inspecting and conferring under glowering skies as the English summer betrayed the summer game. The modern generation is less inclined to react so reticently. It wants something for its money, even if that something isn't always value. It also knows the worth of the newspapers as an ally when it comes to putting pressure on those who, in its less than humble opinion, are doing it wrong. While there may be no such thing as bad publicity in the eyes of publicity seekers, to the marketing-minded men at the TCCB, bad publicity is anathema. Like bad weather. Refunds or not, the Board still has to meet the many and considerable costs involved in a Test match day, and this is something not always appreciated by the public.

Six months after the débâcle at Edgbaston the TCCB announced at its winter meeting that it would offer refunds to ticketholders on that infamous second day, provided they could prove they were not made aware of the regulations concerning refunds at the time of purchasing the tickets. This reflected, a TCCB spokesman said, a moral responsibility which was understood at the time. Which begged the question why, if this moral responsibility was understood at the time, it was not acted upon at the time. Moral sense theory, after all, distinguishes between right and wrong by the feelings of pleasure or pain aroused in the spectator by his perception of events. The events at Edgbaston left the spectators feeling particularly pained, especially the two gentlemen from Wales who were in the toilets at the time the two balls were bowled. For them the pain was all the greater in that, presumably, it followed some sensation of pleasure.

The Board's decision, sadly, had all the appearance of expediency (as in 'conduciveness to the need of the moment' rather than 'desirableness'). It followed immediately upon a ruling in a Birmingham court which found in favour of five trading standards officers who had taken out an action against Warwickshire County Cricket Club on the grounds that they had not been advised of the TCCB's refund regulations when they bought their tickets over the phone by credit card. It was obviously deemed better, and probably cheaper, to offer the refunds rather than lodge an appeal against the judgement, perhaps losing it, and run the risk of additional unwelcome publicity. But underlying the Board's moral responsibility was concern for its highly advantageous advance booking scheme, which brought in thousands of pounds well in advance of each match.

If the TCCB was thinking of investing in moral responsibility, there were also other issues to which it could turn its attention, and these were just as much in the public eye. Across the way at Lord's, MCC had found itself facing a mutiny by a handful of pesky members who were unhappy, *inter alia* and *inter se*, about David Gower's omission from the England team to tour India and Sri Lanka early in 1993. They felt that their club, with its world-wide reputation, was just the vehicle to lead a well-publicized protest about the England selectors' treatment of their hero. Their club, or at least its committee, thought otherwise, ostensibly because the Special General Meeting for which the members had petitioned would cost a lot of money – £17,000 and rising was mentioned in despatches. There was also the possibility of some of the committee, including the president, having to indulge in a spot of self-flagellation on account of their connections with the Test and County Cricket Board. Consequently the committee brought out its big guns: two previous presidents, one a field-marshal, the other a law lord, as well as the current president, a former headmaster at a public school. They were men of authority accustomed to getting their way in their chosen worlds; they did not get it this time. What should have been an exercise in compromise and conciliation, in diplomacy, went deliciously awry. The rebellious members went away neither with their heads tucked underneath their arms nor their tails between their legs. It was a bad day for the Establishment; it had demonstrated what could be achieved by the application of democratic rights. It also made one regret that Ealing's claim to fame in 1992 rested with not much more than being the residence of Neil Kinnock, one-time leader of the Labour Party and two-time loser in general elections. The Lord's affair had the makings of a classic comedy.

It was not the stuff of moral responsibility, though. That lay elsewhere, residing in an issue which called into question how the Test and County Cricket Board took its responsibility as a trustee of cricket. Come to that, it called to account the attitude of the English to matters of moral responsibility in the 1990s, when the newspapers found it more profitable to concentrate on personalities rather than philosophies. A letter to *The Times* from another headmaster, David Jewell, the Master of Haileybury, illustrated the extent to which the TCCB had a responsibility beyond its own commercial confines.

Sir,

I was one of the MCC members who signed the petition which led to the calling of the meeting at Lord's on Tuesday. My signing of the petition did not derive principally from the selectors' decision to omit David Gower. There may be factors involved in that decision of which I am unaware, though it is certainly one which is almost inexplicable.

My principal reason for signing the petition was my very considerable anger at the selection of the South African rebels. I am a strong supporter of contacts with South Africa and greatly regretted the ICC's decision to ban any English cricketer who went to South Africa to coach and play as a private individual. That seems to me an intolerable interference with people's liberty and freedom.

What I criticised at the time, and still do, were the actions of a group of cricketers, collected together in conditions of subterfuge and deceit, undertaking a tour against the express wishes of the government of the day, the cricket authorities in this country, and every other Test-playing country, and, I genuinely believed at the time, the majority of cricket lovers; and all that solely for financial gain.

I do not believe that to be a good example to the young. I find it hard to uphold standards of loyalty and sportsmanship when the England selectors show a gross disregard for such virtues.

It made one pause to consider why the MCC members' petition had not received a more sympathetic hearing from an MCC committee headed by Dennis Silk, the president of the club and, as a distinguished Warden of Radley College for some years, an upholder of high standards.

If cricket is to have a conscience, it is MCC rather than the TCCB that looks the better equipped to exercise it. It has a history of decision-making to refer to; its thinking need not be clouded by the concerns of providing the daily bread, which often colours debate within the TCCB. As a club with a tradition valued and envied around the world, MCC has a reputation that transports it outside the game of cricket itself and positions it within British life. The TCCB, on the other hand, has never been more than a sporting administrative body. Nothing in its past, and it is a recent past, shows it equipped to be an impartial arbiter of right and wrong in the world of cricket. Sometimes, it seems, it struggles to come to terms with what is right and wrong in the *game* of cricket.

In theory, English cricket should not need a House of Lord's to act as the conscience of its House of Commons, because the Test and County Cricket Board, contrary to a common belief, is not the governing body of cricket in the United Kingdom. That authority is the Cricket Council, which was set up in 1968 comprising the MCC, TCCB, National Cricket Association (NCA), the Minor Counties Cricket Association and the Irish and Scottish Cricket Unions. Originally, the Council was constituted so that no one body could outvote the others, with the MCC, TCCB and NCA having five votes each and the Minor Counties one; the Irish and Scottish Unions did not have a vote. But in 1983 the Cricket Council was reconstituted so that the TCCB now had eight votes, the NCA five and MCC three, while the Minor Counties, though continuing to be represented, lost theirs. With the chairman of the TCCB also taking the chair at the Cricket Council, and having the casting-vote that went with the office, the Cricket Council thus ceased to be the independent authority that was envisaged when MCC brought it into being. Its power had been ceded to the Test and County Cricket Board.

It might be asked why MCC should have a say in cricket's affairs anyway. Whereas the TCCB has responsibility for county cricket, Test matches and England tours, and the NCA represents the interest of club cricket and schools cricket – the game at the grass roots – MCC remains a private members' club. It has always had a seat on the TCCB, as have the Minor Counties and Oxford and Cambridge Universities; many of its leading members sit on TCCB committees. Its voice, therefore, can still be heard. But as a voice that influences how cricket in the British Isles is governed, and even how it is played, MCC with each passing year has become increasingly inconsequential. It is infinitely more advantageous to the TCCB to have its own committeemen on the committee of MCC, owner of Lord's Cricket Ground, than it is to MCC to have committeemen involved in the day-to-day affairs of the TCCB.

Originally, MCC had shared power in the Cricket Council because, for the best part of 200 years, it had been the ruling body of English cricket. It was also the copyright holder of the Laws of Cricket, and through its tradition and its traditional provision of the chairman and secretary of the ICC, it played a unique role in the cricket world. MCC had, moreover, been responsible for the Cricket Council, although its reason for establishing it had more to do with those two dubious conspirators, politics and money, than with cricket. Harold Wilson's Labour government in the 1960s had set up a Sports Council for the purpose, among other things, of distributing public funds to sport through the relevant governing bodies. But cricket's *de facto* governing body was a private club whose president was not even elected by its members. In the eyes of a Labour government it was hardly an appropriate repository for public money, even though its responsibilities included many areas outside the boundary of first-class cricket. Indeed, as recently as 1965 MCC had set up the MCC Cricket Association to co-ordinate the variety of functions that now come under the umbrella of the National Cricket Association.

To a national game on more than nodding terms with penury, the prospect of government assistance must have seemed to MCC as appealing as donkey-drop bowling to a schoolboy batsman. In place of runs in the book it saw money in the bank – and for the best intentions, such as coaching and youth cricket. But it made a similar mistake to the schoolboy batsman. 'For a long time, the new "democracy", to which MCC had in a sense sold its birthright, attracted precious little in the way of government funds. But the die had been cast and there was no going back.'* MCC had taken its eye off the ball and been bowled.

At the time MCC relinquished its authority to the Cricket Council Gubby Allen was its treasurer, by tradition one of the most powerful officers of the club. Among his ten predecessors in the 137 years prior to his election in 1963 could be numbered two viscounts, two lords and the immortal Sir Spencer Ponsonby-Fane, who held the treasurership from 1879 until his death in 1915 at the age of ninety-one. Allen, knighted in 1986 for his services to cricket, did not remain in office that long, but even after retiring as treasurer in 1976, at the age of seventy-three, he continued to have an influential role in the affairs of the club as a committeeman and a trustee. Like Sir Pelham Warner, who had proposed him first for the Middlesex committee and then for the MCC cricket committee, he devoted his life to cricket, giving back much more to it than he could ever have taken from it as a player. Consequently, his decision in the autumn of 1982 to resign as one of MCC's representatives on the Cricket Council was an indication of a great unease at the way the administration of English cricket was heading.

In Allen's opinion, the Council, as the governing body of English cricket, should have reflected all levels of the game; his concern was that the realignment of votes within the Council effectively put it in the power of the Test and County Cricket Board, the body whose principal concern was the professional game and raising money to support that professional game. But it needs to be remembered also that MCC had been his power base, an essential part of his political life in cricket. He had been, according to Jack Bailey, who was secretary of MCC during Allen's treasurership and after, 'absolutely unerring and instinctively clever when it came to keeping himself in the centre of what was going on'. Now, with the diminution of MCC's influence, he began to shift towards a different centre.

To insiders, the politics of Lord's during the 1980s can be as intriguing and just about as unfathomable as those, say, between

* Jack Bailey. *Conflicts in Cricket*

the Treasury and the Foreign Office are to anyone interested in the working of government. They were also representative of a time when 'The tensions between old and new institutions, between national traditions and international competition, between conservation and development [were] now evident in all Western countries'.* Nor is an analogy between MCC and the Foreign Office totally without foundation, for in the nineteenth century Ponsonby-Fane had been private secretary to three Foreign Secretaries. The picture of a body of men bound by its own loyalties and networks depicts either establishment with equal facility. To outsiders, however, Lord's power-playing has often seemed little more than a maze of petty intrigues and irrelevant jealousies between two bodies who appeared to be one and the same thing, a fair enough assumption given the number of men wearing TCCB hats and MCC ties. As often as not, to the outsider's ear, they spoke with the same tongue a language steeped in the institutions that had formed them: public school, university (predominantly Cambridge), the Services and the City. But like all closely observed worlds, Lord's breaks into fragments of self-interest and sectional interests.

The dichotomies can seem contrary. Jack Bailey, who as an assistant-secretary of MCC had been responsible for marketing and public relations, areas much concerned with the health of the professional game, went on to become the club's eleventh secretary, while his fellow assistant-secretary, Donald Carr, who captained and managed MCC touring teams, became the first secretary of the Test and County Cricket Board. Carr, whose introduction to first-class cricket was for England against Australia at Lord's in the 1945 Victory Test, had spent his life in the game, going back to Lord's in 1962 as assistant-secretary after captaining Derbyshire since 1955. Everything in his past pointed to his becoming secretary of MCC, but his future lay elsewhere. It may be speculation, but it is unlikely, had Carr been secretary of MCC, that an MCC president would have returned to his City office

---

* Anthony Sampson. *The Changing Anatomy of Britain* (Hodder & Stoughton, 1982)

expressing his astonishment that the club's secretary not only spoke during a committee meeting but also voiced opinions of his own. However, Bailey, the secretary in question, was servant to no man while at the same time being a devoted servant of the club: '. . . none of Bailey's ten predecessors strove more whole-heartedly to guard and uphold what he has deemed to be the rights and privileges of the club.'* His career, prior to his joining MCC, was in business and part-time journalism, and it would have seemed apposite had he, rather than Carr, moved to the newly created TCCB, a body which by its very nature would have to be run on business lines.

My impression of Bailey, albeit more from observation than close acquaintance, was of a man of loyalty rather than a man of ambition. Unlike many of his generation, coming of age as Britain's influence in the world declined and its economy staggered from crisis to crisis, Bailey put his loyalty to his twin institutions, cricket and MCC, ahead of personal interests. There is a feeling when you go to Lord's, a friend remarked, that little has changed, and lulled into a sense of security by this thought people take refuge from what is happening in the world outside. Jack Bailey, I believe, sought to preserve that special feeling for members and public alike, only to become a victim of the commercial clique which, having the counties in thraldom, sought to impose their influence over Lord's. As he wrote in *Conflicts in Cricket*, 'Now, corporate entertainment, the erection of as many advertising signs as possible, and the sale of vast quantities of booze would be the main source of income. The new wave was upon us.' The Test and County Cricket Board wanted uniformity throughout its operation and Bailey, fighting for the independence of MCC, stood in its way.

'With your intelligence and my experience,' Allen once said to Bailey, 'MCC will achieve its rightful place in the game.' But as Allen's influence waned within MCC, their relationship changed. Bailey became aware of traditional courtesies no longer being observed. Contrary to custom, for example, neither the secretary

---

* E. W. Swanton in *Barclays World of Cricket*

nor the treasurer was sought for his advice before A. H. A. Dibbs, the president for 1984–85, chose his successor, and it has since been alleged that Dibbs's nomination of George Mann was made at Allen's instigation. Mann had been chairman of the TCCB from 1978 to 1983, 'in many ways . . . the oddest figure who could possibly be found to head any organisation seeking to demote the Marylebone Cricket Club'.* Like his father, F. T. Mann, he had captained England on each of his Test appearances – five in South Africa in 1948–49 and two against New Zealand in 1949 – and until Christopher Cowdrey led England in one Test against West Indies in 1988, the Manns provided the sole instance of father and son captaining England. He was a popular captain, with a gift for leadership that helped his MCC side travel through South Africa unbeaten. But the interests of the family brewing business claimed his time. Even his captaincy of Middlesex was restricted to just two seasons, 1948 and 1949, when they finished third and equal first in the County Championship. In later years, as a committeeman, he served the county in a number of capacities, being at various times and sometimes simultaneously honorary secretary, chairman of cricket, chairman and president of the club, and he held a regular place on the MCC committee. Indeed, Mann's propensity for high office brings to mind the old saw about Wykhamists. 'Once given a ladder they will climb to the top without questioning its purpose.'

Mann, however, was not a Wykhamist, he was an Old Etonian like Gubby Allen. The Wykhamist in the woodpile was Sir Anthony Tuke, a Scots Guardsman like Mann and a scion of one of the old Quaker families whose ascent to high position in Barclays Bank 'has always been relatively easy'.† Sir Anthony's father, known as 'the Iron Tuke', was chairman of Barclays from 1950 to 1962; Sir Anthony himself, said to be 'less steely', was chairman from 1973 until 1981. He had been nominated as president of MCC for 1982–83 by Hubert Doggart, who had been a few years behind him as a boy at Winchester and had followed him to

---

* Geoffrey Moorhouse. *Lord's* (Hodder & Stoughton, 1983)
† Julian Crossley and John Blandford. *The DCO Story* (Barclays International, 1975)

Cambridge, while his own nominee was a fellow-banker, Alex Dibbs, who had been deputy chairman of the National Westminster Bank from 1971 to 1982. Dibbs, as we have seen, nominated George Mann, by which time Tuke had become the club's chairman of finance.

For Bailey, forced to fight a rearguard action in the battle for Lord's, and conscious that Allen was now antipathetic towards him, the choice of Mann as president must have presented disturbing possibilities. In Dibbs, the beleaguered secretary had found an understanding ally in his struggle to preserve MCC's independence in the running of Lord's. Mann, on the other hand, had such close ties with the TCCB that Bailey felt duty bound to point out to the new president the conflicts of interest inherent in his holding so many offices. Even MCC's legal advisers had 'pointed up the dangers of anyone wearing more than one hat during commercial transactions, in which both protagonists were represented by the same person'.*

Whether or not Bailey recalled it at the time, it was not the first time that Mann's variety of interests had featured in his life at Lord's. When Bailey joined MCC as an additional assistant-secretary in 1967, the club was in its first operational year of a twenty-one-year catering contract worth £12,500 a year but 'with no review clauses and no built-in escalation of rent, and no share of the profit or of the turnover'.† The company with whom MCC had agreed this contract in 1965 was Watney Mann, of whom George Mann, then a member of the MCC committee, was a director. Another regular MCC committeeman about this time, J. S. O. Haslewood, also held directorships in the Watney Mann group. Bailey, of the opinion that the catering lease awarded to Watney Mann was not in the best interests of MCC, eventually renegotiated it on terms more favourable to the club. He was also to reveal his business acumen in negotiations with the BBC for television rights, lending weight to the impression that his talents would certainly have been an asset had he gone to the Test and County Cricket Board.

* Jack Bailey. *Conflicts in Cricket*
† Ibid.

Mann's successor, J. G. W. Davies, took the presidency of MCC from brewing back to banking, while maintaining a Cambridge connection. It had been at Cambridge that Jack Davies made something of a name for himself when, in the University's match against the 1934 Australian tourists, he bowled Bradman for nought, the first time Bradman had failed to score in England. Not that this made any difference to the Australians, who went on to win by an innings and 163 runs. A director of the Bank of England, Davies had succeeded Allen as treasurer from 1976 to 1980, and for his successor as president he nominated a former captain of his old school, Tonbridge, and of his county, Kent. It was a romantic choice for MCC's bicentenary year, and a natural one. Had not Michael Colin Cowdrey's father chosen names that gave him the initials of the world's most famous cricket club?

Cowdrey, moreover, was England's most capped cricketer – only Boycott had scored more runs in Tests – and for many he epitomized everything MCC stood for: good manners, fair play, service to cricket. In his autobiography he had written of his sadness at the way cricket's administration had changed with the establishment of the Cricket Council and with the lessening of MCC's role in the game. 'I view it all with some misgiving, and wonder whether the commercial conglomerate into which it appears to be developing can ever have quite the same family touch again.'* Others, closer to the game, had observed his ambition, socially and within cricket, and among the power players he was well connected. David Clark, the MCC treasurer, had as Kent's captain given him his introduction to county cricket; the chairman of finance, Sir Anthony Tuke, had been the chairman of his employers, Barclays Bank International, when he retired as a player; Sir George Allen, the grey eminence, had been chairman of selectors as he established his place in the England team and became vice-captain to Allen's protégé, Peter May. He gave no indication, however, of being a hit-man, and yet it was during his presidency that Bailey's opposition to the TCCB's encroachment at Lord's was at last eliminated. Four months after Cowdrey took

---

* Colin Cowdrey. *M.C.C. The Autobiography of a Cricketer*

office, Bailey's position as secretary had become so untenable that he was left with no option but to tender his resignation. At the same time, MCC also received the resignation of its treasurer. Clark's integrity, remember, was such that while negotiating for the ICC in the Packer days he had felt it impossible to remain on the committee of Kent, who were fielding several World Series players.

In the conflict that followed, some members used the occasion of the 200th Annual General Meeting in May 1987 to express their disquiet about MCC's relationship with the TCCB, even though Cowdrey, who was in the chair, had written to all members in an attempt to explain the club's position and the circumstances leading to the resignations of its treasurer and secretary. Harder to explain was the reason why the club's solicitors had withdrawn support for the Annual Report – 'Having given and sought opinions on the proper procedure for the Annual General Meeting, they found that matters had gone beyond a point where, in all conscience, they could support the committee in the line it was taking'* – and to Cowdrey's confusion the AGM refused to adopt the Annual Report and Accounts.

In July the committee tried again, this time supplementing the Annual Report with a memorandum dealing primarily with the two conflicting views of MCC's relationship with the TCCB. The first view recognized that the TCCB had, since 1968, been responsible for running first-class cricket in the United Kingdom and that MCC should foster good working relationships with it and be flexible in dealing with it as long as the rights of MCC members were protected. The opposing view saw the TCCB as seeking to encroach upon MCC's authority at Lord's. The memorandum pointed out to members that the relationship between MCC and the TCCB had been deteriorating, and that there was a real risk of at least one major match being taken away from Lord's. However, the committee believed that one of its major duties to members was to preserve a full programme of matches at Lord's and it was confident that, with improved understanding and trust

* Jack Bailey. *Conflicts in Cricket*

between the secretariats of MCC and the TCCB, recognition of the Board's overall responsibility would not cause serious difficulties.

This time, with postal votes to support it, the committee won the day. The soft centre held sway, voting for what had been presented to them as their own interests. But in the years that followed, the hard facts of commercial life exercised MCC more and more as its influence in the affairs of the game grew less and less. Sir George Allen did not live to see the sponsors' logos that appeared on the outfield at the Nursery End – not in front of the Pavilion, for the time being – or the grossly coloured run-stealers flickering to and fro on Sunday afternoons. But if the members of MCC thought that in acquiescing in 1967 they had saved their rations of big-match cricket, events elsewhere meant they might be made to think again. Across the river, south of the Thames, Surrey were forging ahead with a redevelopment plan to make The Oval the equal of Lord's, if not its master. A new battlefield was opening up, promising a campaign to be fought between the traditions of Lord's and the facilities at The Oval. If MCC were left with little option but to make further concessions to the Test and County Cricket Board, it would be a grim reward for selling its birthright in order to sustain the game it had ruled for almost two centuries.

12

The Soft Option

Throughout 1987, while the resignation of its secretary reverberated around the St John's Wood coffee-houses, the Marylebone Cricket Club celebrated its bicentenary as if nothing untoward had happened in its cul-de-sac of power. Members and guests danced and dined at exclusive functions, sufficiently removed from the public gaze to leave them unaware that *hoi polloi* were taking no notice at all. Memorabilia were struck to mark the occasion, and offset costs, and in August a match was played between MCC and a Rest of the World XI. This the public could attend, and if the paying attendance over the four days (on the fifth day it rained) failed to better that of an above-average day or night at Melbourne, receipts in excess of half a million pounds were especially welcome to the club. It had, after all, to guarantee the Test and County Cricket Board something in the region of a quarter-million pounds for the right to celebrate its 200th birthday with a cricket match on its own ground. This was, apparently, compensation for the Test match that the TCCB might have staged at Lord's between England and Sri Lanka. Give or take the odd inflationary point, however, someone somewhere had done his sums correctly, for the following year this fixture brought in receipts of just under a quarter of a million pounds.

The composition of the two sides for the Bicentenary match, while bringing together many of the world's best cricketers, was noteworthy for the absence, initially, of any South African players. The great attraction would have been their legendary left-handed batsman, Graeme Pollock, but by restricting selection to players currently engaged in county cricket or from Test-playing countries, MCC was avoiding the possible embarrassment of withdrawals by players from countries hostile to South Africa. In the event Clive Rice, the Transvaal and Nottinghamshire captain, was called up for the MCC side to provide one of the club's oldest friends with at least one representative.

Given MCC's dual role as England's premier cricket club and as the secretariat of the ICC, South Africa had been a thorn in its paw for a number of years. And if there were times when it looked as if MCC members would rather cut off the paw and throw away the rest of the body, the club's and the game's administrators had nevertheless come to terms with the reality that sport could be divorced from politics no more than politics can be divorced from everyday life. That had been pointed out in 1958 by a member of the club who happened at the time to be prime minister of the United Kingdom.

'Nothing we do in this small world can be done in a corner or remain hidden,' pronounced the man who helped hand over the remains of an empire and in later life accused his political heirs of selling off the family silver. 'It is our earnest desire to give South Africa our support and encouragement, but,' Harold Macmillan told the two Houses of the South African Parliament in his famous 'Wind of Change' speech, 'there are some aspects of your policies which make it impossible to do this without being false to our deep convictions about the political destinies of free men, to which in our own territories we are trying to give effect.' The South Africans gave him an ovation, proving if nothing else that they should have stuck to sport rather than get involved in politics. By the end of the next decade, as far as cricket was concerned, they had been blown away, a haven for platitudes and politicians – if that isn't tautological – but not for cricketers.

It all began, as every schoolboy knew before politicians moved out of sport and into education, with the D'Oliveira affair. Basil D'Oliveira was a South African-born cricketer who had travelled to England to further a cricketing career denied him in his own country because he was not white. He was a Cape Coloured. The affair began towards the end of the 1968 season as soon as

D'Oliveira was not included in the MCC team selected to tour
South Africa that winter. Having seen him in action in the West
Indies in 1967–68, I was less surprised than some who had seen
him play only in England, whether for England or for Worcestershire, although arguments based on his effectiveness overseas
carried little weight in the emotive discussions of the time. In the
five Tests in the Caribbean he had scored 137 runs for an average
of 22.83, something of a let-down after averaging 42.66 in his
first series, against West Indies in 1966, and 83.00 and 50.00
against India and Pakistan respectively in 1967. He did, however,
average 40.10 for the tour, with a highest score of no more than
68 not out, playing in all but one of the twelve first-class games.
So while it was true that he had had a disappointing tour from
the point of view of the Tests, it was by no means disastrous
overall. And subsequent overseas tours with MCC sides illustrated
that he was adequately equipped for conditions other than English
ones. In Pakistan in 1968–69 he averaged 53.66 in the three Tests,
and as an ever-present in Illingworth's Ashes-winning side in
Australia in 1970–71 he averaged 36.90, including a century at
Melbourne. His Test batting average abroad was 37.72 against
an average of 41.35 in England.

Perhaps it is too cynical to think that his poor performance in
the West Indies was welcomed in some quarters. Comments from
South African government ministers, including Prime Minister
Vorster, during 1967 had done nothing to clarify the position of
an MCC team if it were to include D'Oliveira for a tour of that
country. MCC could not omit him on the grounds that his colour
made him unacceptable to their hosts, as New Zealand had omitted Maori players, as recently as 1960, from their All Blacks team
which went to South Africa. Indeed, as Denis Howell, the British
minister with responsibility for sport, had informed the House of
Commons early in 1967, almost two years before the scheduled
tour of South Africa, MCC had advised the government 'that the
team to tour South Africa will be chosen on merit'. Should any
player chosen be rejected by the host country, the tour would be
called off. What it boiled down to, in simple terms, was this. If
the tour was to go ahead, its fate was secure only if D'Oliveira

was not in the side. And if D'Oliveira was not in the side, it had to be for cricketing reasons, not political ones. It stood to reason that D'Oliveira's cricket in 1968 was going to come under avid scrutiny, and his selection, or non-selection, for the tour was always going to attract controversy.

In January 1968, on the advice of Howell, MCC wrote to the South African Cricket Association for an assurance that the team would be accepted as selected. When no reply came, MCC heeded the wisdom of its immediate past-president, Sir Alec Douglas-Home, and did not press the issue by making further enquiries. Reaction rather than action was the watchword: choose the team and see what happens. Denis Howell may have known how to blow a whistle on the football field, but Sir Alec, a member of the MCC committee, had been Foreign Secretary. He knew the score, and it wasn't played on a whistle. It was the sound of silence. Mr Harold Pinter, who appropriately became an MCC member that year, frequently incorporated it in the plays he wrote.

A play drawn on the events of 1968, as they involved Basil D'Oliveira, would require a playwright with an aptitude for the absurd. Straight, it would be much too confusing. D'Oliveira began the 1968 Test series against Australia as a member of the England team for the First Test at Old Trafford, where he remained unbeaten with 87 in the second innings. England were beaten by 159 runs. No one else in the side passed fifty in either innings but, says *Wisden*, 'the value of his belated effort was difficult to appraise. England needed him as an all-rounder and he had failed as a first-change bowler.' His figures, incidentally, were 25–11–38–1 and 5–3–7–1, which if not penetrative were Scrooge-like in their economy. They hardly constituted failure. Still, all things are relative, relativists would have us believe, and if you believe that you can believe anything. On the other hand, belief in anything helps a lot in l'affaire D'Oliveira. Because after top-scoring at Manchester, poor Dolly was left out of the twelve at Lord's in favour of another all-rounder, Barry Knight, who was reputed to get the odd delivery past the bat. In the circumstances – greenish pitch and overcast conditions – Knight did more than that, taking three for 16 in fewer than eleven overs as Australia

were bowled out for 78 in their first innings and made to follow
on. The weather helped them save the game.

To get the structure of this play right, it need not be chronologi-
cal; at this point the playwright could introduce, either as narrator
or Greek chorus, the England captain, Colin Cowdrey. 'I saw
D'Oliveira as a batsman who could bowl well.' A reason for all
seasons. But if that was the case, why had D'Oliveira been chosen
at Old Trafford as the first-change bowler? Against West Indies
in 1966, his eight wickets cost 41.12 apiece; in 1967 his three
against India cost 29.66 and his one wicket against Pakistan 85.00;
in 1967–68 his three wickets in the West Indies series came at
97.66 each. Indeed, prior to the Manchester Test he had hardly
bowled that season and had taken only four first-class wickets.
His forte was deceptive medium-pace swing bowling that was
well-suited to breaking partnerships; it needed no deep insight to
know that he was not a first-change Test match bowler. So what
did the selectors have on their minds when, from their appointed
fourteen at Old Trafford, they omitted three specialist bowlers in
David Brown, Tom Cartwright and Derek Underwood, leaving it
to D'Oliveira, the batsman who could bowl well, to support Snow
and Higgs?

What with one thing and another,* it was not surprising that
D'Oliveira's batting went off the boil. And as he was thought of
as a batsman, albeit one who could bowl well, that put him out
of the running for the Test team at a time when England were so
desperate for batsmen that for the Leeds Test they brought Ted
Dexter in out of the cold after a few warm-up games for Sussex.
(A nice part for Nigel Havers there.) They also gave debuts to
Roger Prideaux, to open in the absence of the injured Boycott,
and Keith Fletcher, to the ire of the Yorkshire crowd, whose own
Phil Sharpe had been in the fourteen called to Headingley. Poor

---

* As was disclosed by the *Sunday Times* in April 1969, D'Oliveira received in July
1968 an offer of employment in South Africa as a coach and sports organizer for
non-Europeans. Made on behalf of the South African Sports Foundation by an
employee of Rothmans in South Africa, the offer was for 'five or ten years' at £4000
a year plus a house and a car, but it had to be taken up before the MCC side for
South Africa was chosen. The reason was obvious: acceptance of the offer and his
return to South Africa would rule D'Oliveira out of selection for the touring team.

Fletcher made their day with several Very Nearly catches at first slip which the Yorkshire crowd, knowing how Sharpey would have swallowed them, never forgot about afterwards. 'Gnome' crowned his misfortunes by being caught behind without scoring when England batted.

This was all very well, except that England were still one down in the series with one Test to play and they could no longer win back the Ashes. But then cricket has always had a logic of its own, as Wittgenstein might have discovered had he spent some time at Fenner's during his Cambridge days. He might also have revised his thinking on logically private language, in which, it is said, all words must be defined in terms of the logically private experience of the individual language user. He would have been just the man to have on hand when, out of nowhere, Basil D'Oliveira returned to the England team for the final Test. Although summoned to The Oval in case England needed a medium-pace bowler, D'Oliveira actually came into the side as the replacement for an unwell batsman, Prideaux. But then his very presence at The Oval owed everything to others' misfortune. Cowdrey's first two choices as his reserve bowler, Cartwright and Knight, had gone the way of all flesh when called upon to play five days at The Oval and golf on Sunday. They were not fully fit. D'Oliveira, however, was not only fit but in fine bowling form, even if some of the *cognoscenti* were a trifle sniffy about the pitches on which he was getting his wickets. Without recourse to *Wisden* or Wittgenstein, it's a fair assumption that Cartwright and Knight had been taking their wickets in similar conditions.

Although D'Oliveira's bowling was to be a factor late in that Oval Test, it was his batting that gripped the nation's attention and exercised the selectors' minds. Sustained by John Edrich's fourth hundred in thirteen Tests against Australia, England after winning the toss were 272 for four at the end of the first day, with Edrich 130 not out and D'Oliveira 24 not out. Next day they continued their partnership to 121 before Edrich was out for 164, with England's score 359 for five. Their final total was 494, to which the remaining batsmen, Knott, Illingworth, Snow, Underwood and Brown, contributed 51 runs. The balance came from

D'Oliveira. Dropped behind the wicket early in the morning, when 31, he dominated the Australian bowling for most of the day before being last out for 158, and as he walked back to the pavilion the crowd rose to him in an emotional response to his glorious comeback and to his innings. Not only had he put England in an impregnable position from which to advance towards victory; in everyone's minds – bar one or two – he had played his way into the touring team for South Africa. Even Cowdrey thought so. 'They can't leave Basil out of the team,' he told Jack Bailey as they drove back to Lord's on Tuesday evening. 'Not now.'*

Perhaps Cowdrey was overcome by the euphoria of a dramatic victory, won with six minutes to spare after a thunderstorm on the stroke of lunch on the last day had threatened to thwart England. Australia were 86 for five, 265 runs in arrears, but if they thought the weather had saved them again they had not reckoned on the patriotic efforts of the groundstaff and volunteers to mop up the water. The sun became a willing ally to England's cause, and at a quarter to five Inverarity and Jarman followed the England team on to the field to resume the struggle. They had resisted for just over half an hour when Cowdrey called on D'Oliveira, and with the last ball of his second over he hit the top of Jarman's off stump as he stretched forward. It was the breakthrough England needed. Immediately Cowdrey brought back Underwood at the pavilion end, and in his first over Mallett and McKenzie fell to catches by David Brown in the leg trap. The second, a marvellous effort, exemplified the England players' commitment and let loose all their tension and excitement. Gleeson stayed with Inverarity before Underwood bowled him as the game moved into the last quarter-hour, and finally, after keeping England at bay for four hours, Inverarity padded up to a straight ball from Underwood and was leg before. In twenty-seven balls kicking and spitting on a drying pitch, many of them beyond the comprehension of the Australian batting, the England left-armer had taken four wickets at a cost of just six runs.

That evening Cowdrey sat down at Lord's with the England

---

* Jack Bailey. *Conflicts in Cricket*

selectors and MCC officers to choose the team to tour South Africa. Next day, when the names were announced, D'Oliveira's was not among them. For the purpose of the tour, explained chairman of selectors Insole, he had been regarded by the selectors as a batsman pure and simple, as distinct from an all-rounder. There were places for Prideaux and Fletcher, neither of whom played at The Oval, but none for the returning hero. The only sound louder than the cries of conspiracy was the sigh of relief blowing out of South Africa. But it was a premature sigh. They had forgotten the wind of change. Among the fifteen – another fast bowler was still to be included – the selectors had picked Cartwright in expectation of the 'seamer's paradise' which the Australians had encountered in South Africa in 1966–67, but which Cartwright in his fitter moments had not found conspicuous two years earlier. If anything, his selection was something of a punt, for it depended not only on grassy pitches but also on Cartwright's fitness. That summer he had missed taking 100 wickets for the first time in seven years, a shoulder injury and various strains keeping him out of eleven Championship games for Warwickshire. He had not played in a Test all summer; in fact, the last of his five Tests had been against South Africa on his home ground, Edgbaston, in 1965.

Wittgenstein would have enjoyed the reasons given for Cartwright's selection as much as those given for D'Oliveira's omission. All of them, it was stressed, were *cricketing* reasons. But heaven knows what he would have made of the final scene. When Cartwright was ruled unfit, and had to withdraw from the touring team, the selectors brought in not another bowler to replace him but Basil D'Oliveira, the man they said they had not regarded for the tour as an all-rounder. It was all too much for the South Africans. They had been conned by Macmillan ten years earlier; now they could recognize a conspiracy when they saw it. D'Oliveira's inclusion had to be politically motivated; why else would their friends at Lord's replace a bowler with a batsman? There was no cricketing sense in that. Having a South African-born player from beyond the pale was . . . well, it was beyond the pale. The tour was cancelled. The curtain came down on the drama, leaving most of those attending it as much in the dark as they had been throughout.

D'Oliveira's omission could have been a conspiracy, it could have been a cock-up. I used to favour the former: conspiracy theories were, after all, a growth industry in the 1960s, and it did emerge later that in March 1968 a former president and treasurer of MCC, Lord Cobham, was given to understand by South Africa's Prime Minister Vorster, 'that it was extremely unlikely that Basil D'Oliveira would be acceptable to the South African government as a tourist, if selected by MCC'.* Lord Cobham told Billy Griffith, the MCC secretary, in April of his meeting with Vorster, and Griffith in turn told the MCC president, A. E. R. Gilligan, and the treasurer, Gubby Allen. All three were present at the selection meeting which chose not to include D'Oliveira in the MCC team for South Africa. Moreover, when you look at D'Oliveira's Test career, in which he played forty-four times for England, he missed just four Test matches between 1966 and 1972. Three of those were in 1968 against Australia. There is certainly potential there to support a conspiracy theory. On the other hand, after twenty-five years of living in England, I'm inclined to put some money on the cock-up.

---

* MCC Statement, 10 April 1969

13

Rands and Rebels

So many and so tangled were the divisions engendered by the D'Oliveira affair, and the cancellation of the MCC tour to South Africa, that arguments and opinions continued to be exchanged beyond autumn into the winter. Indeed, sufficient members of MCC were concerned about the events of the summer, and about the future policy of English cricket towards South Africa, to call a Special General Meeting of the club. It was held in December at Church House, Westminster, where these three resolutions were debated:

1. That the members of MCC regret their committee's mishandling of affairs leading up to the selection of the team for the intended tour of South Africa in 1968–69.
2. That no further tours to or from South Africa be undertaken until evidence can be given of actual progress by South Africa towards non-racial cricket.
3. That a special committee be set up to examine such proposals by the SACA towards non-racial cricket; the MCC to report on progress to the Annual General Meeting of the club; and to the governing body for cricket – the MCC Council.

The Rev David Sheppard and Mike Brearley, England captains past and future, spoke in support of the resolutions, arguing that South Africa, in organizing its sport on political grounds, 'intrudes its politics upon all teams which visit the country'. The committee's view, advanced by two future presidents of the club, Aidan

Crawley and Dennis Silk, was that MCC's role was to foster cricket wherever it was played, and not to interfere in the internal affairs of governments or governing bodies. It was a sound establishment principle, espoused by a pair well suited to pressing establishment suits: Crawley had been a member of parliament for both the Labour and Conservative parties, while D. R. W. Silk rejoiced in the third name of Whitehall. Not surprisingly they won the day. Less than sixty years had elapsed since the British government passed the Act of Union, which, in addition to bringing together the four provinces of the Cape, Free State, Natal and Transvaal, deprived South African Blacks of the vote.

Moral issues for the English often seem to the outsider to be a matter of private concern rather than of public conscience. In that way they can be safely relative, instead of requiring an understanding of right and wrong. Many saw support for South African cricket as support for friends who supported Britain in two world wars. These friends were white. However, many Cape Coloureds also wore the King's uniform in the two world wars, having earlier worn the Queen's uniform in the Boer Wars. Yet since the election of the National Party in South Africa in 1948, the Cape Coloureds had not only lost their right to play cricket against white men and boys; most importantly they had lost the right to vote and the right to live and love where and whom they pleased. It was not simply and solely a matter of politics; it was a matter of humanity, and this transcended cricket. At least it should have.

But as events in South Africa have shown, as the country edges towards democracy or anarchy, and perhaps both, nothing in that country is clear-cut. By the 1970s the government that had refused to accept Basil D'Oliveira as a member of an MCC team in 1968, was admitting non-white sportsmen into the country – and it is conceivable, just, that if D'Oliveira had been of Indian or West Indian birth, other than South African, he might have been allowed entry in 1968–69. Eventually, well in advance of the developments of the early 1990s, he did go back to South Africa, to coach white and Coloured players, and at the same time earn the censure of the South African Committee on Sport for being a 'turncoat renegade on the isolation of apartheid South African sport'. He had, they accused him, 'betrayed the aspirations of millions of oppressed sportsmen by disagreeing with SACOS's code on sport'.

To its everlasting credit, South African cricket did make progress towards non-racial sport, most spectacularly by taking cricket into the black townships. In the 1970s, multi-racial teams were put out in opposition to the teams taken to South Africa by Derrick Robins, and to the International Wanderers managed by Richie Benaud. Common to both tour parties was the presence of the Kent and West Indies all-rounder John Shepherd, and the Pakistan and Surrey batsman Younis Ahmed. In addition, a non-white team competed, with government permission, in the domestic Gillette Cup limited-overs competition. A new non-racial body, the South African Cricket Union, was formed in 1977, and in 1978 the Cricket Council in England accepted that South Africa had met the requirements set down for its return to Test cricket. That same year, despite opposition from India, Pakistan and West Indies, the ICC agreed to send a delegation to South Africa to examine their progress. Headed by the president of MCC, Charles Palmer, in his capacity as chairman of the ICC, it contained representatives from Australia, England and New Zealand, all friends of South Africa, and at the 1980 meeting of the ICC the South African Cricket Union was asked to make written submissions to support its readmission to the international body. Hopes were high in the republic for an end to the years of isolation and for a resumption of Test cricket; they were hopes falsely raised.

When it came to it, neither Australia nor England, co-founders with South Africa of the ICC, was prepared to propose South Africa's readmission, and the first move had to come from a founder member. Neither was prepared to upset relations with India, Pakistan and West Indies, whose governments opposed all dealings with South Africa, conveniently disregarding the multifarious incidents of trade between South Africa and the rest of the world, including India and many of South Africa's neighbours. Not even invited into the conference proper, the South African delegates were reduced to arguing their case outside it, stressing what had been achieved in fulfilling their obligation to the development of multi-racial cricket. They could even offer an assurance that the

South African government intended to exclude sporting bodies
from the conditions of three laws which had hindered the spread
of multi-racial cricket. It was all to no avail. Instead of readmitting
South Africa, the ICC gave full membership, and so Test-match
status, to Sri Lanka, whose election in 1965 to associate membership had been signalled by a letter to *The Cricketer* asking why
the United States of America, granted associate membership at the
same time, had been put on a par with Ceylon in the cricket world.

'What more can we do?' asked Rashid Varachia, the Bombay-
born president of the South African Cricket Union. But he had
been involved for long enough in South Africa's attempts to gain
recognition to know that there would be no answer. At one time
he had been refused a visa by the Australian government to visit his
son there, because of his involvement with South African cricket.
Formerly a president of the South African Cricket Board of Control, the administrative body for Indian and Coloured cricketers,
Varachia found continually frustrating the unwillingness of some
ICC members to discuss South Africa and so come to understand
its many and complex problems. But he was a frail man, working
under the handicap of a heart complaint, and ICC's rebuff of
South Africa in July 1981 proved to be his last disappointment.
He died that December, by which time plans were under way
within the South African Cricket Union to answer what had been
a plea as much as a question.

Knowing there was no more they could do, aware that their
opponents would be satisfied only with political change that was
beyond cricket administration's scope, the South African authorities took a leaf out of Kerry Packer's book and hired themselves
a touring team. To the consternation of the Test and County
Cricket Board, the team was not only English but contained four
players – John Emburey, Graham Gooch, John Lever and Derek
Underwood – who had just returned home from England's tour
of India and Sri Lanka. A fifth, Geoffrey Boycott, had also been
on that tour, only to return to England after the Fourth Test
pleading 'physical and mental tiredness'. At New Delhi, during
the Third Test, he had become the leading run-scorer in Test
cricket, passing Sobers' record of 8032 runs, and had equalled the

England record of twenty-two Test centuries, previously shared by Cowdrey and Hammond.

Although the presence of any England players was a blow to the moral standing of English cricket, Boycott's was especially bitter. It was not just that he had been involved in setting up the tour. His selection for the England team for India in 1981–82 – along with that of the Northamptonshire captain, Geoff Cook – had threatened the tour's very existence because they had already played in South Africa. Cook had captained Eastern Province the year before, but ten years had passed since Boycott played a first-class game in the republic. Only when both had expressed their repugnance to apartheid did Mrs Gandhi, India's prime minister, allow the tour to proceed.

'In retrospect,' said Walter Hadlee, a former captain of New Zealand and at the time president of the New Zealand Cricket Council, 'cricket – indeed all sport – should be deeply indebted to Mrs Gandhi and her government: in expressing continued opposition to the discriminatory laws of South Africa, and at the same time taking the view that sportsmen and supporters should not be penalised, India has set an example which, if followed, could solve many of the problems confronting cricket in particular and sport in general.'* He had in mind, no doubt, England's experience in Guyana earlier in 1981, when Robin Jackman was refused a visa because of his South African connections. However, Boycott, in selling what remained of his talents to South Africa, had told the Indians what they could do with their example, and they did not forget.

Seven years later, when Gooch was due to lead an England team to India, the Indian government refused to grant visas to eight members of the side, including the captain, and the tour was cancelled. The Indians' objection to the eight – Rob Bailey, Kim Barnett, Graham Dilley, Emburey, Gooch, Allan Lamb, Phil Newport and Tim Robinson – was on the grounds that their names appeared on a so-called United Nations list of sportsmen who had links with South Africa. Yet their policy of refusing visas ran

* *Wisden Cricketers' Almanack 1982*

counter to the ICC's principle that no country should be allowed to influence the team selection of another. And it left India open to charges of hypocrisy in that four of the unacceptable eight had been allowed into the country the previous year for the World Cup.

Gooch, however, had not been captain when England competed in the 1987 World Cup, in which they reached the final only to lose to Australia. He had, on the other hand, captained the rebel England team that slipped into South Africa in February 1982. It was asking a lot of the Indians to accept him now as captain of an official England team, particularly as it was known that Gooch had originally intended to play in South Africa for Western Province, rather than tour India. He had changed his winter plans when offered the England captaincy, whereupon Western Province released him from his obligations to them. The appointment as vice-captain of Emburey, another rebel of '82, served only to enforce an impression that England's selectors were short on sensitivity as much as common sense. But, shades of the D'Oliveira affair, they explained that their brief was to select the best possible team from the cricketing point of view. 'We don't pick teams for political reasons,' said their chairman, Peter May.

He had a point, however naïve his statement sounded at the time. Even in cricket, politics was a science ever changing. Who would have forecast that, four years later, Gooch would again be selected to take an England team to India; an England team, moreover, containing not just Emburey but two other players who, along with Emburey, had been banned for touring South Africa during those intervening four years? If that wasn't strange enough for the short-term time traveller, when Gooch's team arrived in India, their hosts' leading players were still involved in a Test series in, of all places, South Africa.

Gooch and Emburey, fellow-rebels and close friends, were not the only survivors of the 1981–82 tour returning to India eleven years later. Keith Fletcher, England's captain then, was returning as team manager, an appointment viewed with trepidation not only in Yorkshire but also by critics of the Gooch–Stewart regime, which ended with Stewart's retirement earlier in 1992.

Fletcher had been Gooch's mentor at Essex, and it was feared he would oversee an extension of the grind-over-Gower methodology. Fletcher in India had presided over a dreary series of six Test matches which realized only one positive result, although it is overlooked by many who were not there that he was a popular captain. He did not deserve to have his brief stewardship undermined by the conspiracy being planned within the team.

Once India had won the First Test of the 1981–82 series, at Bombay, any result other than a draw in the remaining Tests was going to be difficult on pitches tiresomely true and lacking in bounce. At Bangalore, New Delhi, Madras and Kanpur, the first innings was still in progress on the final day of the match. In their captain, Sunil Gavaskar, India had a batsman technically equipped to shut England out and a strategist never shy of slowing the game down by means of the over-rate. England's response was equally negative, when instead it required something out of the ordinary to snatch the initiative. In the Fifth Test, at Madras, Gooch was inspirational in reaching fifty off forty-six deliveries and his century off 139, but it took him more than three valuable hours after India had batted into the third day. It was all academic anyway: when Gooch walked off that evening, still unbeaten with 117 against his name, Chris Tavaré, opening with him in place of the now-departed Boycott, was 26 not out on his way to scoring 35 in five and a half hours. In an innings almost twice as long, ten and a half hours, Gundappa Viswanath had posted 222 for India and partaken in a three-man stand for the third wicket which brought 415 runs. In this time, it was estimated, the population of India increased by some 75,000. Word of Tavaré's marathon would have put them off Test cricket for life.

In stark contrast to the pitches provided for the remainder of the series, the First Test pitch at Bombay produced uneven bounce and, for the fourth successive Test at the Wankhede Stadium, a result in four days. When England played there in 1980, to celebrate the Golden Jubilee of the Board of Control for Cricket in India, they had won handsomely, swept to victory by Botham's century and thirteen wickets. It was the first time anyone had achieved the double of a century and ten or more wickets in a

Test match. Twenty-one months later, he bowled unchanged throughout India's first innings at Bombay, taking four for 72 from twenty-eight overs, and he finished with match figures of nine for 133. But it was not enough. England managed only 166 in their first innings after Boycott and Tavaré had extracted 92 runs out of fifty-nine overs for the second wicket. Then nine wickets fell in two and three-quarter hours, which destroyed any faith the England team might have had in either the pitch or the umpires. Needing 241 to win, with time not a factor, they were bowled out second time round for 102, the lowest total made by any touring team in a Test in India. Kapil Dev and Madan Lal shared the ten wickets evenly in twenty-five overs and two balls, and India won by 138 runs.

Fletcher was an old India hand: he had been there with Tony Lewis's side in 1972–73, Tony Greig's side in 1976–77, and an International team, captained by Micky Stewart, in 1967–68. He knew the ropes, he knew the tricks. He also knew that the umpire's word was final, and he instilled in his team the importance of accepting the umpiring for what it was. So it was a sad irony when Fletcher himself snapped, knocking the stumps askew with his bat after being adjudged caught at the wicket on the second day of the Second Test at Bangalore. He subsequently wrote a letter of apology to the Indian Board, but that moment of frustration was to count against him when Peter May took over as chairman of selectors the following March.

The decision to dump Fletcher as England's captain, taken, no doubt, for good cricketing reasons, came back to haunt the selectors for the rest of the decade. In his touring team of sixteen, Fletcher had two recent captains of England in Boycott and Botham; indeed it had been Botham's defeats in two series against West Indies and his eventual succession by Mike Brearley halfway through the 1981 Ashes series that had precipitated the situation that led to the appointment of Fletcher. But it would transpire that his side also contained five of the six men who captained England at some time in the next seven years: Bob Willis, David Gower, Mike Gatting, John Emburey and Graham Gooch. Chris Cowdrey, who toured India with Gower's side in 1984–85, was the absentee. Of these five, it was Gooch, the last to be chosen, who emerged as an outstanding leader of men and as a respecter of cricket's traditions.

It is idle to speculate how England's Test decade would have unfolded had Gooch not gone to South Africa immediately after that 1981–82 tour of India. But a look at his record prior to that shows how important his batting had become. In 1979–80 he was England's leading run-scorer on the tour of Australia and India under Brearley, and at home in 1980 he was the leading scorer against the West Indians. His 123 at Lord's, one of only two hundreds by England in that series, was an astonishingly authoritative display by a batsman who had gone for thirty-five innings without recording his maiden Test hundred. Driving with supreme confidence and getting quickly into position to hook or pull, he hit a six and seventeen fours in a stay of just over three and a half hours. When he was lbw to Holding a quarter of an hour before tea, he had scored virtually 75 per cent of England's runs in a total of 165 for two. Tavaré, who had joined Gooch when the score was 20, was becalmed somewhere in the twenties at the time of Gooch's dismissal, and he was almost five hours roaring into the forties, where he finally foundered.

The following spring Gooch returned from the West Indies having headed the aggregates for the Test series with an average of 57.50, and he was the leading run-maker for the Tests and the tour in India and Sri Lanka in 1981–82, this time with an average of more than 50. Only the Australians in 1981 had found his measure. They had blighted his England debut at Edgbaston in 1975 by dismissing him for a pair, Marsh catching him behind the wicket in both innings. He lasted three balls first time out and seven the second time, but as *Wisden*'s editor sympathized, 'he was only one failure among so many in a nightmare situation'. Caught out on a wet wicket after Denness – in what was unsurprisingly his last match as England's captain – put the Australians in first, England were dismissed for 101 and 173 and beaten by an innings and 85 runs with a day and a half remaining. Walker and Thomson were Gooch's executioners then; in 1981 his principal persecutors were Lillee, Lawson and Alderman, keeping the ball to a full length and moving it late. After five Tests he was averaging just 13.90 – his career Test average at the time was 33.33 – and England dropped him for the Sixth Test at The Oval. They also left out Gower, who was having a similarly unsatisfactory series.

For what it was worth, Gooch was also the leading run-scorer for the anything-but-official England side he captained in South Africa in 1981–82. The rebel tourists' averages were headed by Dennis Amiss, whose England career did not survive his defection to the Packer camp in 1977. His England playing career, that is. In 1992 he was a member of the England Committee which, in addition to the infamous omission of Gower, selected Gatting, Emburey and Paul Jarvis for Gooch's side to India and Sri Lanka. All three had been serving a five-year exclusion from international cricket for touring South Africa in 1989–90, in disregard of the ICC regulations on sporting contacts with that country. But they were lucky. The ban was lifted after two years, following South Africa's readmission to the ICC in 1991. Like the Master of Haileybury, I question the probity of the selection. Sadly, the election to the England Committee of a two-time apostate leaves me with no confidence in the Test and County Cricket Board when it comes to matters of right and wrong.

To say that Gatting, Emburey and Jarvis, from time to time a fast bowler for Yorkshire, had served their sentence is simply not good enough. They took their money and ran, knowing that they would not be able to play Test cricket for their country (or the TCCB's exclusive version of it) for at least five years. That the ban ended early was good fortune to add to the fortune they had stashed away as the reward for their desertion. 'It is axiomatic,' Jim Swanton once wrote, 'that a game reflects the character of those who play and those who serve it.' Amiss went to Packer and South Africa; Gatting and friends went to South Africa; they all put hard currency before country. This may not matter to some people, but those who say this have to think again when they decry the way cricket is run by the Test and County Cricket Board. The two issues are not easily separated when the rights and wrongs of English cricket are debated – not in themselves, perhaps, but in the standards on which decisions are based. Although bright new ideas may reform the game superficially, improving its image, as it were, the deep-rooted problem, the attitude of many cricketers to the game, has remained untouched.

For cricketers to defend their defections with the excuse that they are professional sportsmen exercising their right to earn a living presents a narrow, self-centred view of narrow lives. It refuses to acknowledge that there is a world beyond the world of cricket to which they, both as professionals and sportsmen, owe something if only an example. At the same time it lays open to question their real motivation when playing for their country, if their country – as opposed to *playing* for their country – means so much to them that they would willingly deny themselves the right to play for it. Rights, invariably hard won by someone else, can be easily lost if they are not respected.

When Gatting and his cohorts went to South Africa in 1989–90, it was not the statistics of their forsaken Test careers that came to mind, but the following statistics from a more serious conflict.

Out of the eight or more serious strikes in the aircraft industry between February and May 1943, for instance, six were over wages; one because of objection to an efficiency check on the use of a machine; and one because of objection to two fitters being transferred by management to a different section in the same shop. The remaining twenty-eight stoppages in this period were caused by such questions of overriding importance in the midst of a total war as arguments over piece rates; complaints about canteen facilities; the alleged victimisation of a shop steward; the use of females in riveting work; the refusal of Amalgamated Engineering Union members to work with non-union employees; a refusal of management to allow collections for the Red Army during working hours; and a sit-down strike to prevail on other workers to join an embargo against payment by results.*

* Correlli Barnett. *The Audit of War* (Macmillan London, 1986)

In percentage terms of output, of course, those stoppages were as minimal as Gatting's contribution to England's misfortunes in 1989 against Australia. They were trivial, they were parochial. But they did come at a time when Britain was at war. None the less many of those workers no doubt felt that they were exercising their right to withdraw their labour, just as those who went to South Africa in defiance of the ICC regulations exercised their right not to play for their country.

Whereas the players Gatting took to South Africa in 1989–90 knowingly went in defiance of the game's governing body, Gooch and his colleagues in 1981–82 broke no law. It would be naïve to suggest that they did not know their going would be opposed: the secrecy with which the tour was arranged is evidence of that. Playing or coaching in South Africa as an individual had never been prohibited by the English authorities, as they would be by the ICC dictate of 1989 which Gatting's team flouted. But visits by a team were not countenanced, even though in the 1970s, as we have seen, private tours did take place. The Cricket Council in 1973 had not been prepared to approve a visit to South Africa by the winners of the Gillette Cup, stating that they felt it would infringe the spirit of the declaration in 1970 that no Test tours involving England and South Africa would take place until South African cricket was played, and their teams were selected, on a multi-racial basis. The difficulties which confronted Botham's team in Guyana, and Fletcher's side prior to its India tour, were sufficient to show how attitudes overseas had hardened against any contact with South Africa.

For going to South Africa unofficially, Gooch and his team were banned by the TCCB from selection for England for three years. It was acknowledged by George Mann, the chairman of the Board, that 'The players have broken no law, none of our rules.' The TCCB was not trying to punish them, he said, it was merely 'taking the minimum steps needed to protect cricket'.

Earlier, at its 1982 spring meeting, the Board had been warned of the financial implications to English cricket if that summer's tours by India and Pakistan were jeopardized. There was also the World Cup, scheduled for 1983 in England, to be taken into account. The chairman of the Indian Board of Control had wasted no time in letting it be known that India's visit to England depended on a firm line being taken against the 'rebels', and the threat of lost revenue concentrated the minds of the TCCB wonderfully. It was obvious to all members that three years was exactly the right length of time for a suspension. It got them past the potentially lucrative World Cup, and also past the next tours to India and Pakistan. Gooch, God willing, would be available for the 1985 home series against Australia, but until then England would have to do without him and his co-conspirators. As in so many things it was all a matter of compromise, and Gooch had put himself in a compromising position. However, it gave a hollow ring to the ICC's statement later in the year that *on no account* should there be political interference by one country in the selection of the team of another. They had obviously forgotten the power of the profit and loss account.

14

The Rule of Essex Man

Michel de Montaigne, in his Essays, recounts a story from Plutarch in which a visitor to the studio of the artist Apelles stands for some time without speaking. Eventually, however, he begins to discuss the artist's work, only to earn this reproof from Apelles. 'While you were silent, you appeared to be a man of outstanding merit, with your decorations and your fine clothes. But now we have heard you speak, there is no one in my shop, not even the simplest boy, who doesn't have a poor opinion of you.'

Being unable to remain silent, when silence is the best course, is a predicament for sportsmen as well as politicians in these days of a demanding media. Some word, however lacking in wisdom, must be extracted. It saves the interrogator from the subsequent embarrassment of expressing an ill-conceived opinion; it also presents the sportsman, or the politician, with an opportunity to put his foot in it. We have not matured to such a degree that we can resist the temptation to topple heroes.

So when David Gower remarked after England regained the Ashes under his captaincy in 1985, 'I'm sure West Indies will be quaking in their boots at this moment,' he was more than tempting fate, albeit whimsically. He was revealing a flip side of his personality which sat uncomfortably with the mental discipline required of a Test-match captain. He was hinting at a lack of *gravitas*. Similarly, Ted Dexter's comment that Graham Gooch had about as much charisma as a wet fish told us more about the man who was to head the England Committee than it told us about the man who would lead England out of the international wilderness.

For the South African government, Basil D'Oliveira's inclusion in the
1968–69 MCC team to tour that country was beyond the pale.

Players in the politics of power. *Clockwise from top left* Sir George 'Gubby' Allen, *eminence grise* of English cricket; Donald Carr, first secretary of the TCCB; Jack Bailey, the beleaguered secretary of MCC in the 1980s; Doug Insole, a driving force as chairman of the TCCB.

Colin Cowdrey at Canterbury in 1965: Kent captain, England cricketer.
A life given to the game was recognized by his knighthood in 1992.

Chesterfield *(above)* and Abergavenny, in their individual ways, evoke the unique place that cricket has in the landscape of British life.

Same game, different hemispheres, but in truth a Lord's cup final is a world away from a day/night game beneath the Melbourne lights.

Left Tony Greig and Kerry Packer, protagonists in the cricket revolution that became World Series Cricket, leave the London Law Courts on the first day of the hearing in 1977 when the new world took on the old – and won.

Below Ten years after, and Lord Home of the Hirsel, a former president of MCC, reminds fellow-members of happier days during a dinner at the Guildhall which formed part of the club's bicentenary celebrations.

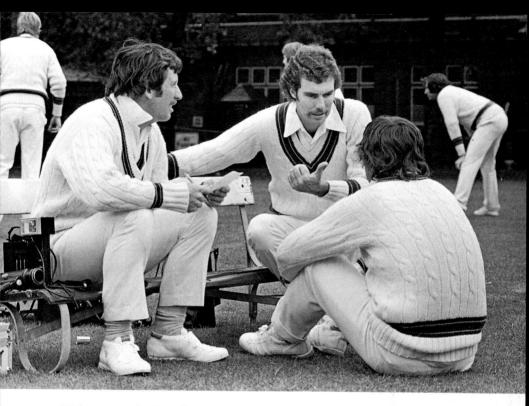

High command – Ian Chappell *(left)*, brother Greg and Rod Marsh plot
England's downfall in the mid-seventies.

Shock trooper – Jeff Thomson welcomes forty-one-year-old Colin
Cowdrey back to Perth and Australia in his own inimitable way.

Not content with the writing on the wall, by the 1990s cricket's marketing men were making their mark wherever possible – and the field of play seemed as good a place as any. 'It is a symbol,' the editor of *Wisden* wrote in 1992, 'of the level to which English cricket has to go to earn a crust.' The TCCB was not amused.

Principis est virtus maxima, nosse suos, Martial claimed. 'It is the chief virtue of a prince to know the people about him.' This was Brearley's strength as a captain; it was also Gooch's, for all that it was badly overlooked by many when, in two Tests in 1988, he indicated that he was the one England cricketer of Test-match quality best suited to captain his country. The only England player to appear in every Test that summer – the selectors called on twenty-three players for the five Tests against West Indies – Gooch came to the captaincy by default, as it were. But few were prepared, or able, to see beyond the received wisdom: Gooch was a morose, self-contained individual given to periods of introspection. It did not help that he had taken over when Chris Cowdrey was forced to withdraw because of injury, Cowdrey's elevation beyond his means having been greeted in some quarters, with an embarrassingly orgastic manifestation of joy, as the second coming. 'We believe Cowdrey's style of leadership is what is now required,' said the chairman of selectors, Peter May, when naming his godson as England's captain for the Fourth Test against West Indies, proving yet again the value of the silent sound bite.

Cowdrey, previously capped five times on Gower's tour of India, never played for England again, except unofficially as a disillusioned and disgruntled rebel in South Africa. At Headingley he had taken over from John Emburey, whose two-Test term in charge saw England beaten by 134 runs at Lord's and by an innings and 156 runs at Old Trafford – a drubbing which threw into doubt the motivation as well as the ability of some England cricketers. The two defeats also gave short shrift to theories that, had he not gone to South Africa in 1981–82, Emburey would have been a potential heir to the England captaincy by virtue of his succession to Brearley as captain of Middlesex. Instead the Middlesex captaincy had gone to Mike Gatting, and it was Gatting who had begun that 1988 series as England's captain, despite evidence in Pakistan and New Zealand the previous winter that nature had meant him to be a corporal rather than a captain.

Gatting's style was to lead by example, and this told against him as an England captain. For a county captain, among cricketers he knew and young players in awe of his record and rank, example and experience can be enough. But captaincy of a selection, as an England side is, requires an intelligence that knows how to draw on players' limitations as well as their strengths. It is all too easy to assume that because a cricketer has a reputation he has gained it by merit; that is not always the case. Similarly, just because good fortune has raised a man to high office, it does not follow that he is wise.

In the field, when a situation called for conjuring, Gatting was coercive instead; when the tide of events turned against him, his response was untimely anger rather than considered patience. Hands on hips, puffing petulantly, he made a good teapot. Like Gower, he was unfortunate in having come through the ranks to captain his peers, for he never gave the impression of being more than their equal when he needed to be more than that to warrant their respect. It is not enough – Montaigne again – 'for those who govern and command us . . . to have a common understanding, and to be able to do the same as we can. They are very much below us, if they are not infinitely above us; as they promise more, so they have to perform more.'

When England fell foul of the umpires in Pakistan in 1987–88, Gatting was incapable of seeing beyond the apparent injustice. Tom Graveney's defence of Gatting's contretemps with umpire Shakoor Rana – 'Pakistan have been cheating us for thirty-seven years and it's just getting worse and worse' – may have struck a chord, probably C, in many English breasts, but it ignored more than cricket's code of the umpire's word being law. It overlooked an essence of English cricket that appears to be a weakness and is in fact its great strength: there is more to the game than the game itself. 'We are going to see certain things in the Australian game which are not to their detriment but which are not in our game,' Percy Fender told an audience in London in 1926. 'We are up against a lot of things which we don't do but which other people do.'*

Understanding that, and accepting it, was a mark of Englishness. It did not mean lying down and being walked over. It meant being

---

* Richard Streeton. *P. G. H. Fender* (Faber and Faber, 1981)

better; being above winning and losing. Gooch understood that. When, in the Lahore Test, England opener Chris Broad refused to leave the crease after being given out, adjudged caught at the wicket, it was Gooch who went down the wicket and persuaded him to go. This quiet authority presented a side of Gooch often camouflaged by his public image of apparent diffidence. Since the end of his ban for going to South Africa he had expressed a reluctance to touring, preferring to spend time with his family, and when he stepped down from the captaincy of Essex in 1987, after just two seasons in charge, his critics felt vindicated in their estimate of him as anything but a team man. They could not have been further from the truth.

Gooch had a nightmare summer in 1987, having the year before led Essex to the County Championship title. The enthusiasm he displayed, and his bold approach in his first season as captain, had augured well for Essex, although justifiable fears were expressed at the time that the batting was heavily dependent on Gooch's ability to give the innings a sound base. These fears were realized in 1987, and Essex slumped to twelfth in the Championship. Gooch had not gone to Australia with Gatting's successful side in 1986–87, opting understandably to be at home to help with his young family, and he was under some pressure to regain his England place. After getting Essex's Championship defence under way with an imperious 171 off 206 balls against Gloucestershire at Bristol, however, he came to grief in May. His first four innings at Chelmsford, against Warwickshire and the visiting Pakistanis, produced a double pair; and though he came into the England side for one of the three one-day internationals when Gatting was injured, he missed the entire five-match Test series against Pakistan. By the end of the season he had dropped himself to the middle of the Essex order. So strong is the memory of Gooch's desultory batting that summer that it comes as a surprise to look in *Wisden* and see he headed his county's averages with 1100 runs at 39.28.

For some years now, Gooch had infuriated the purists with his upright stance at the crease, the bat held aloft as the bowler approached. He in turn could point to the volume of runs he scored, and to the important fact that he was comfortable with this method. There were times, watching him from side on, when I was surprised how limited his footwork was, often being little more than an adjustment of a position taken up ahead of the popping crease. It may have been why he was susceptible to bowlers operating on a close wicket-to-wicket line. Gooch looked as if he was positioned for the ball slanting or swinging into him from outside the off stump: instead of having to move to the pitch of the ball, he was already there to drive or work it through mid-wicket. In other words, he had devised a method to cope with the type of bowling and the vagaries of pitches commonly found in County Championship cricket.

A century against Nottinghamshire late in May 1984 illustrated how good Gooch's technique and temperament were when the conditions favoured the bowlers. Latecomers to the county ground at Chelmsford, seeing Gooch at the crease with few runs to his name – and having read in their morning newspapers that he had been not out overnight – would have been forgiven for thinking they had missed nothing by staying at the office until noon. Play must have started late, though it was a fine morning. As it was, Essex had lost their remaining nine wickets for 33 runs in just over an hour, principally to Clive Rice and Kevin Saxelby. They were following on, 171 runs in arrears, and Gooch was still coming to terms with the excellent bowling of Richard Hadlee and the eccentricities of the pitch. Anything on his stumps he was already forward to and covering with the broad face of his bat; when the ball seamed or swung away he didn't follow it but remained inside the line, albeit looking badly beaten if the ball moved late. Here, until lunch, was a fascinating duel between two cricketers embarking on outstanding seasons. Hadlee, the New Zealand all-rounder, would finish that summer with 1179 runs and 117 wickets, the first man to achieve the double since Fred Titmus in 1967 – and there was more first-class cricket in Titmus's day. Gooch, still under suspension from England selection, would become the first player for eight years to top 2500 runs in a season, beating in the process Jack O'Connor's record Essex aggregate of 2308 runs which had stood for half a century.

That Thursday morning, as Hadlee consistently and persistently

tempted the edge of his bat, Gooch would nod bucolically to his
adversary, a measure of acknowledgement, go forward to tamp a
disturbed divot, then shamble back to his mark and take up his
stance. Occasionally Hadlee was treated to an almost smile, as
Gooch recognized he had been saved by good fortune rather than
his good judgement, and Hadlee would paddle back to his mark
with a wan smile playing on his own lips. Both, it was apparent
from the boundary, were having the time of their lives, enjoying
every moment of a tussle deserving of their talents. In the afternoon
the pitch eased a little and Gooch went on to the second of his
eight first-class hundreds that summer. Next morning Hadlee captured five wickets in five overs for 11 runs and Nottinghamshire
won by ten wickets. It gave them something to look back on when,
on the last day of the season, Essex headed them at the top of the
County Championship table by a margin of fourteen points.

In 1985, his ban over, Gooch was an automatic selection for
England, and in the six Tests against an Australian side itself a
victim of defaulters to South Africa, he scored 487 runs at an
average of 54.11. Such was the run-glut that England's batsmen
feasted on that summer, three men scored more: Gower 732 runs
at 81.33, Gatting 527 at 87.83 and Robinson 490 at 61.25.
Gower's aggregate was a record for England in a home series
against Australia. Until the final Test Gooch had been somewhat
overshadowed by his fellow-opener, Robinson, but at The Oval
he batted throughout a gloriously hot first day as England established the position that was the foundation of their innings victory
and their regaining the Ashes. With the captain, Gower, whose
double-century had set up the innings victory at Edgbaston in the
previous Test, Gooch added 351 for the second wicket in just over
five and a half hours. Next morning he moved from 179 to 196
before Australia's best bowler, Craig McDermott, brought off a
stunning caught and bowled to dismiss him. Pulling up abruptly
in his follow through, McDermott had to throw himself to his
right to hold on to Gooch's mistimed drive just inches from the
ground.

It was not half as stunning, though, as the dismissal that ended
Gooch's comeback innings in 1987. The Essex captain's indifferent

form had kept him not only out of the England team that summer but also out of the MCC Bicentenary match, for which he might have been an obvious choice a year earlier. However, when New Zealand and Somerset's Martin Crowe had to withdraw from the MCC team, Gooch replaced him. He did not open, but batting at number three he was soon in action, Broad being lbw to Imran Khan for 10. Action, perhaps, is the wrong word, for Imran and Courtney Walsh worked Gooch over mercilessly in the early stages as he tried to establish his innings. Gooch's problem, the unkind said, was in his head, but truth be told his body was going as much as his head. Where once he had been an oak, rock solid as in that encounter at Chelmsford with Hadlee, all summer long he had been a poplar, swaying in and out of line as the bowler ran in. In itself his upright stance was not flawed, but stillness is a primary tenet of batting, and Gooch had forsaken it.

Gradually, however, on that bright blue day at Lord's, Gooch moved out of the shadows into the sunlight. He ceased stooping, he stopped swaying. He stood upright, kept his head still and let the ball come on to his bat. Suddenly the old authority was there as once again the ball was punched through the field. He was past his hundred, coming up to five hours at the crease, when he advanced down the pitch to drive the West Indian off-spinner, Roger Harper. It could have been his nineteenth boundary. Instead Harper, all six feet five of lissom limb, swooped and threw down the stumps in one continuous action as Gooch was still carried forward by the momentum of his stroke. So quickly did it happen, it almost deceived the eye; Gooch, momentarily unable to conceal his disbelief, left the ground to a standing ovation, still smiling at the brilliance of Harper's effort. Earlier in the afternoon, just after lunch, Harper had casually plucked out from overhead a ball that would have gone for six had Gordon Greenidge tried to clear most other fieldsmen. Each was a classic example of fielding at its best, but somehow Sir George Allen and Denis Compton contrived to give the fielding award to Clive Rice, for two splendid slip catches completely lacking the sublimity of Harper's magic moment.

That Gooch's poor form was no more than an aberration became apparent later in the year in India and Pakistan, where he was the leading run-scorer in the 1987 World Cup and in the three Tests that England played against Pakistan. His 115 from 136 deliveries against India in the World Cup semi-finals was one of the memorable innings of the tournament: no great respecter of spin bowling, he literally swept England into the final by his demolition of India's two slow left-armers, Maninder Singh and Ravi Shastri. But he did not go with the England side to Australia and New Zealand after Christmas, when his presence would have been a restraining influence on a side seemingly hell-bent on confirming the impression of the Englishman abroad as a lager lout. 'England teams have prided themselves on maintaining certain standards,' wrote Alan Lee, who reported the tour for *The Times* and *Wisden*. 'Should this principle be sacrificed, the game would be on a course inevitably ending in the gutter.'

Time may show that Gooch's greatest contribution to English cricket was not the number of runs he scored but the sense of pride he brought back to the England team. If not exactly lager louts under the management of Gatting and Stewart, England's cricketers were certainly in danger of becoming laager louts. Too many times their demeanour signalled a belief that the world was conspiring against them. But then living in the public eye is not a sinecure; Swift's tax has to be paid, and in the late twentieth century the tabloid press had set itself up as taxman to the nation. 'To tax and to please, no more than to love and to be wise, is not given to men,' claimed Edmund Burke, and few England cricketers in the second half of the 1980s would have pretended that they were pleased with the men of the press. Headline writers hounded Gatting as England's stock plummeted; yet in a supposedly egalitarian age he should have been a champion of the people's papers. Instead he was portrayed to the people as a buffoon. Why?

Do you think we really count? You don' wanna take any notice of what them ole papers say about the workers bein' all-important these days – that's all squit! 'Cos we aren't. Do you think when the really talented people in the country get to work they get to work for us? Hell if they do! Do you think they don't know we 'ont make the effort? The writers don't write

thinkin' we can understand, nor the painters don't paint
expecting us to be interested – that they don't, nor don't the
composers give out music thinking we can appreciate it. 'Blust,'
they say, 'the masses is too stupid for us to come down to them.
Blust,' they say, 'if they don't make no effort why should we
bother?' So you know who come along? The slop singers and
the pop writers and the film makers and women's magazines
and the Sunday papers and the picture strip love stories – that's
who come along, and you don't have to make no effort for
them, it come easy. 'We know where the money lie,' they say,
'hell we do! The workers've got it so let's give them what they
want. If they want slop songs and film idols we'll give 'em that.
If they want words of one syllable, we'll give 'em that then. If
they want the third-rate, *blust!* We'll give 'em *that* then. Anything's good enough for them 'cos they don't ask for no more!'
The whole stinkin' commercial world insults us and we don't
care a damn. Well, Ronnie's right – it's our own bloody fault.
We want the third-rate – we got it!*

Gooch's strength as a man and as captain of England was his
understanding that the press needed him more than he needed it.
Not having openly courted eminence, he ignored the tax demands
and maintained an innate dignity based on his belief of right and
wrong. If he knew he could not ignore the press – accommodating
the media went with the territory that was the captaincy of England – he could at least play the game on his terms, and he played
it better the more he became accustomed to it. There must be more
vigour and strength in the bearer than in the burden, Montaigne
thought, and Gooch, having come to the captaincy initially
through Cowdrey's misfortune, demonstrated that he possessed
both.

After that Oval Test against West Indies in 1988 Gooch con-
fessed, almost in surprise, how much he had enjoyed leading England. He had not, after all, been captaining Essex that season.
What struck me particularly was the positive way England

* Arnold Wesker. *Roots* (Penguin Books, 1959)

approached the match, and the way the England players had responded to Gooch. In a way that hadn't been so obvious since Brearley's day, the captain was definitely in charge. The sometimes-implied philosophy of the interim years – the players are first-class cricketers and they know what England expects of them – was not in evidence. Gooch, one felt, let it be known what *he* expected of them.

England had their best game of the series since the drawn First Test at Trent Bridge where, helped by innings of 73 and 146 from Gooch, Gower's unbeaten 88, plus bad light and rain – more than a day's playing time was lost – England ended a sequence of ten defeats by West Indies. By the third day at The Oval, England's commitment under Gooch had been such that it was looking as if they might even establish a winning position. Batting first, England had been dismissed for 205, but on the second day Gooch's Essex team-mates, Neil Foster and Derek Pringle, bowled to such telling effect that, for the first time in thirteen Tests against West Indies, England took a first-innings lead. Foster produced some outstanding fast-medium bowling to send the first four batsmen back with 57 runs on the board, maintaining an accuracy and hostility that allowed Gooch to keep pressure on the West Indian batsmen. But as at Lord's, where Graham Dilley had reduced the tourists to 54 for five with a first-morning spell of 13–4–35–4, little Gus Logie and the elegant Jeff Dujon helped them escape.

When Gooch and Tim Curtis put on 50 for the first wicket, hopes rose for an England win, only to dip with the evening sun. At the close of the second day, England were 64 for three, a lead of only 86, and on Saturday, after an invigoratingly defiant 34 from night-watchman Foster, the prospects of victory receded. Only Gooch stood firm, as the remainder of the England batting folded against consistent fast bowling from Winston Benjamin and Walsh, essentially the second string of the West Indies pace quartet. He had batted for seven hours two minutes when he was the last man out, for 84, an immense feat of concentration and his longest innings without reaching three figures. With more than two days to score 225, West Indies had no need to force the pace, and in fact won at a canter on Monday afternoon. But England had been rudderless from the second over of their innings, when Gooch damaged his hand trying to hold on to a catch off a no-ball. He took no further part in the game and Pringle, becoming the fifth man to lead England in the series, could not contain a rampant Greenidge or remove the smoothly efficient Desmond Haynes.

England's second innings, with Gooch and Foster contributing 118 of the 202 runs scored, emphasized once again, and it needed emphasizing, the inherent weakness of England's domestic cricket. It was not simply the individual technical deficiencies that let England down; it was the inability of players to sustain concentration while grafting against the odds. So often in County Championship matches batsmen did not have to struggle in the second innings to set a target for the side batting last. Runs were presented to them. At The Oval, no one was able to match Gooch's mental stamina, even though Curtis, Rob Bailey and Robin Smith had shown in the first innings that they possessed the patience and resolution demanded by the second innings. Too frequently in recent years England's Test cricketers had not looked as if they were equipped to play a two-innings game over five days.

As we have seen, England's winter tour of India, with Gooch as captain, was cancelled. What happened next, I believe, set England's Test cricket back twelve months. In the autumn of 1988, Peter May retired after seven years as chairman of selectors, and an idea began to circulate that the time was right for a new style of selection and management of the England team. One influential proponent of such change was the chairman of the Test and County Cricket Board, Raman Subba Row, who wanted to put the management of England's cricket on to a more professional basis. This, it was mooted, would improve the chances of success on the field. Another advocate, this time from outside the Board, was the former England captain, Ted Dexter, who had retained close ties with cricket as a writer and television commentator. He was also involved with the game through his public relations business, and his proposals for a streamlined management of England's cricket carried all the marks of a well-planned campaign. It was not entirely coincidental that Subba Row was also in the

PR game, and around the counties could be heard disturbed murmurs that they were being railroaded into accepting new ways because of the advance publicity being given to them.

Dexter was still something of a favourite in the land. Everyone who was around at the time remembered his cavalier batting and his brave despatching of the fastest bowling. Not all, however, recalled his at times vague captaincy, and perhaps he was equally fortunate that still fewer called to mind some of his public utterances. His judgement was not impeccable. There was, for example, his contention in an article in the *Observer* in 1965 that West Indies' victory over England in 1963 was 'meaningless'. Why? Because in Dexter's opinion Charlie Griffith, one of the West Indian fast bowlers in that series, was a 'chucker'. It had not been the opinion of the umpires, in that Griffith was not called for throwing in 1963, so by implication, if Dexter was right, the umpires had not done their jobs properly. Later in 1965, in the course of a Scarborough Festival match between an England XI and the Rest of the World, he repeated on television his allegation that Griffith, playing in the match, was a thrower, but again the umpires failed to substantiate his claim. While his controversial comments certainly added spice to a friendly occasion, they could scarcely have been what the English authorities wanted put abroad after their successful negotiations to bring the money-spinning West Indians back to England in 1966.

If the announcement in March 1989 that Dexter would lead the new England Committee came as little surprise, I heard it none the less with a sense of foreboding. Based on what I had seen the previous summer of Gooch's leadership at The Oval, and against Sri Lanka at Lord's, I felt that England's best chance lay with him at the helm. I felt similarly sure that an England Committee with Dexter as its chairman would replace Gooch as England's captain. Which is what happened. Although it subsequently came to light that Dexter and Stewart had apparently wanted Gatting for the job – an appointment rightly vetoed by the Cricket Committee chairman, Ossie Wheatley, on account of Gatting's past misdemeanours – David Gower was named to lead England's defence of the Ashes in the forthcoming series against Australia. If that was Dexter's first mistake, his second was to offer a reason for the choice. He was looking to Gower, he announced, to set the tone and style for the team, and by the season's end that statement had been shown to be no more than the empty rhetoric it sounded in the spring. England were humiliated in the six-Test series, losing four–nil and calling upon twenty-nine players in the process. Dexter, however, said he was not aware of having made any errors, an interesting deduction deserving of deconstruction. As the principal error was there for all to see, the problem for Dexter was obviously his awareness.

15

A Matter of Awareness

Whether Ted Dexter used 'aware' consciously or not, with respect to his errors or absence of them, it was an intriguing word-selection. 'Awareness' and in particular its antonym, 'unawareness', have dwelt for a long time in the subconscious of English cricket; in most aspects of English life, no doubt. As often as not, unawareness has been little else but tacit awareness, as an editorial in *The Cricketer* suggested when commenting on the need to examine and rewrite the no-ball law as it related to throwing. '. . . if a relatively simple definition can be found, it would do more than resolve the arguments and ill-feeling about throwing which are apt to crop up from time to time. It would make the periods of "unawareness", such as occurred in the 1950s, less frequent. Any proposals made by MCC about throwing since then, however genuine and valuable, have inevitably carried less weight because English cricket did not keep its own house in order in that period.'*

In more recent times another aspect of the Laws as they relate to bowlers has given the authorities something to think about. Less serious than throwing, in that it does not carry the same risk of physical injury, it has none the less caught the attention of the public – though probably not for cricketing reasons. It is the practice of damaging the surface of the ball so that bowlers – it is claimed – swing the ball more. The New Zealand and West Indian teams that toured Pakistan in 1990–91 both accused the host country's players of tampering with the ball in this way. And in

---

* *The Cricketer*, 4 June 1965

a remarkable admission of malpractice, the New Zealand manager said that one of their bowlers, the medium-fast Chris Pringle, had done some doctoring of his own during the Test match at Faisalabad, where he returned figures of seven for 52 as Pakistan were bowled out for 102.

Imran Khan, who gave the New Zealanders a miss but captained Pakistan in the series against West Indies, described the charges as 'ridiculous . . . The Pakistan bowlers play in county games and have never been accused by any player or umpire. They played under the close scrutiny of John Hampshire and John Holder in the series against India [in Pakistan in 1989–90] and not a finger was raised.' As there were twenty-two leg-before-wicket decisions in the four Tests, this is not strictly accurate, but we know what he means. Or think we do. Neither question nor voice, not even a hackle, was raised.

Imran's defence of his countrymen deserves some scrutiny, however. As Imran himself had not played county cricket in England since 1988, the only Pakistan bowlers with current county experience taking part in the series against New Zealand and West Indies were the two pacemen, Waqar Younis and Wasim Akram. Waqar, in fact, had recently enjoyed a sensational first season at The Oval, taking 95 wickets for Surrey in all cricket. He was the leading wicket-taker in the Sunday League with thirty-one at 12.77 apiece, signalling economy as well as penetration, while in the County Championship he took fifty-seven wickets at just under 24 each. Nor was it his speed and wicket-taking ability alone that held one's fascination in 1990. There was also his accuracy combined with the awesome deadliness of a late-inswinging yorker that threatened batsmen's toes as much as the stumps. To be 'wackered' was a painful experience, whichever way you looked at it. Twenty-nine of his Championship victims were bowled and eight were lbw; the other twenty were all caught by fieldsmen ranged behind the wicket. This was fast bowling in the Statham mould, and Lancashire members must have gazed south with ever-increasing envy as their injury-dogged Pakistani, Wasim Akram, managed just fifteen expensive wickets in seven Championship games and thirty-five in the three limited-overs competitions.

While no one at the time could dispute Imran's claim that neither Wasim nor Waqar had been accused by any player or umpire in county cricket, there was nevertheless sufficient official concern about ball tampering in the county game for the Test and County Cricket Board to take pre-emptive measures against it. At its summer meeting in 1990 the Board increased the umpires' powers with respect to Law 42.5 – Unfair Play: Changing the Condition of the Ball – so that roughing up the surface could be dealt with in the same way as picking the seam. In the playing conditions authorized by the TCCB, the penalty for both offences thus became the replacement of the deliberately damaged ball with an older and inferior one.

It is obvious, then, that the TCCB was aware in 1990 that roughening the ball was going on in county cricket. Its measures to control this were equally apparent, being announced after the summer meeting, and yet several seasons passed before the public was made fully aware of this particular aspect of ball abuse. It was not until the tour of England by Pakistan in 1992 that a sense of righteousness developed about a practice which, if not rampant, was already in existence in county cricket. The absence of any campaigning vigour against ball tampering in county cricket in 1990 or 1991 could, of course, have resulted from unawareness. Unfortunately, giving the matter such prominence in 1992 left the English press open to charges of prejudice against the Pakistanis, rather than concern for the Laws of Cricket. I seem to recall a New Zealand bowler in 1990 working industriously at the seam as he walked back to his mark – but this did not have picture editors screaming for incriminating photographs. Of course he was not making the ball swing all over the place, and New Zealand were not beating England.

What brought matters to a headline was Allan Lamb's allegation in the *Daily Mirror*, at the end of the Pakistanis' tour. 'How Pakistan Cheat at Cricket' the banner blazoned, and within a wink the lawyers were dropping writs at the Grace Gates. It followed upon the umpires changing the ball during England's innings in the one-day international against Pakistan at Lord's in late August. (The Test series, which Pakistan won two-one, had finished a

fortnight earlier.) Lamb, it transpired, had drawn the umpires'
attention to the ball's condition, and as Alan Lee subsequently
reported in *The Times*, 'I understand that the umpires, Ken Palmer
and John Hampshire, went to the England dressing-room during
the fateful lunch interval and reported to the captain, Graham
Gooch, that the ball had been changed because they considered
it had been tampered with. Pakistan's officials had already been
apprised of this in the referee's room.'*

What followed that decision by the umpires was a shambles or
a cover-up and most likely both, with neither the TCCB, which
appointed the umpires, nor the ICC, which appointed the match
referee, prepared to state why the ball had been replaced. A function of the match referee, it should be pointed out, is 'to ensure
that the spirit of the game is observed and the conduct of the game
maintained during Test matches and one-day internationals by
players, umpires and team officials, either on or off the field . . .'
Because neither body would confirm that the ball had been
replaced under Law 5.5, having become unfit for play by losing
its shape or going soft – a frequent enough occurrence – a logical
assumption was that action had been taken under Law 42.5, which
states that 'No one shall rub the ball on the ground or use any
artificial substance or take any other action to alter the condition
of the ball'. What complicated the issue even more was that
the replacement ball was said not to be of 'much inferior condition' to the original, as specified by the TCCB's playing conditions concerning Law 42.5, and the learned friends leapt on this
technicality like pit bull terriers on a kitten. The only certain
conclusion is that cricket's administrators had an awareness
problem.

One of the umpires at Lord's was John Hampshire, whose
unraised finger a year and a half earlier had been called as a witness
in Imran Khan's defence of his country's bowlers. But had his
finger remained unraised at Lord's except for Allan Lamb's irregular intervention – and assuming, of course, that the ball was
changed under Law 42.5 – how reliable is Mr Hampshire's finger

* 29 August 1992

as a witness? What, a learned friend would want to know, had been the awareness of the umpires prior to Lamb's disturbing the Lord's pigeons.

As often happens when uncalled cats make untimely leaps out of the bag, the other unraised finger, that of John Holder, also became more than a footnote in a foreign land. A few days after fining Lamb £5000 – subsequently reduced on appeal – for whistle-blowing his own composition in the *Daily Mirror*, the TCCB let it be known that Surrey had been fined £1000 for several reported instances of ball tampering. It emerged at the same time that these were not all recent misdemeanours. One went back to 1990, when umpires Chris Balderstone and Barrie Leadbeater changed the ball during Gloucestershire's innings at Cheltenham. In 1991, umpires Don Oslear and Bob White took exception to the ball the Surrey bowlers were using against Yorkshire at Guildford, but they could do no more than report the malpractice to the Board, there being no ball of inferior condition available as a replacement. 'Waqar Younis transformed the game', began *Wisden*'s report of the match, 'with a typically devastating spell of fast bowling and, less predictably, struck 31 in nineteen balls to ensure Surrey's second victory of the Guildford week with two balls to spare.' That spell, which wrapped up the Yorkshire second innings, saw Waqar take five wickets for eight runs in four and a half overs.

Waqar, however, was free from association with Surrey's next brush with the Law 42.5, being on tour with the Pakistanis and the object of other allegations. This time Surrey were playing Leicestershire at The Oval, where their dexterity with the ball was not to the liking of umpires Barry Dudleston and John Holder. It all added substance – not that substances needed adding – to a nice little story Vic Marks told in his *Observer* column about 'an abused ball' being handed round at a captains' meeting at Lord's in 1991. 'When it reached David Hughes of Lancashire he gulped as he recognised the evidence. He passed it on to Ian Greig of Surrey who, adhering to the forthright tradition of the family, blurted out: "This looks like one of ours." Apparently,' Marks continued, 'the England team were cautioned during the Fifth Test against West Indies last year.'* That England team contained two Lancashire players, in Phillip DeFreitas and Mike Atherton, and Surrey's Alec Stewart.

The umpire who took a second look at the ball at The Oval in 1991, the Test that England won to square the series against West Indies, was John Holder. It was his opinion that untoward damage had been done to the ball's surface, although the ball was not changed. What was changed, however, was Holder's ranking as an umpire. After four years on the Test match and one-day international panel, he disappeared from it in 1992. Given the Pakistanis' apparent trust in him, expressed in his umpiring there in 1990–91, his omission seemed a trifle odd; in terms of sensitivity it was probably on a par with David Constant's presence on the list for the 1987 series against Pakistan, despite the visitors' request that he did not stand against them.

There is no reason, of course, why Holder should have been on the Test match panel for the series against the Pakistanis in 1992. It is just a pity, in the circumstances, that someone with an awareness of the problem was not asked to stand in a series which, given previous accusations about the Pakistan bowlers, had the potential to be a difficult one. Come to that, I have always believed it to be a pity that in most countries the umpires for international matches continue to be chosen by the home authority. It is all very well to say, as many do, that all umpires are neutral. The home authorities that appoint them are not neutral. So even if he maintains his integrity by stating that his bread is buttered on both sides, the most neutral umpire always knows who provides the butter and the bread. This is no more satisfactory a state of independence than the system prevailing in English cricket whereby the umpire's ability – to all intents, his future career – is judged not by an impartial assessor but by the team captains in the matches in which they stand. We are told that the system works, but whether or not it works for the right reason is an altogether different matter. It was Ted Dexter who said 'it suits the administrators to have umpires where they want them – under their thumbs', but

* 30 August 1992

that was in 1966. It would be worrying if Dexter still had reason to believe that today, just as it would be disturbing to find we were returning to a period of 'unawareness' in order to avoid embarrassing incidents. The TCCB would not want to find itself in the position of MCC in 1965, having to issue statements denying that umpires had been asked to turn a Nelsonian eye to infringements of the Laws.

'In recent months,' said the MCC statement that July, 'reports have appeared in certain sections of the press that first-class umpires were, in 1963, advised by an "influential member of the MCC" not to call C. Griffith of the West Indies for throwing during the West Indies tour of that year. Despite denials that, as far as MCC committee was aware, no such advice or suggestion was given or implied, these reports have persisted, to the detriment of the game. MCC have, therefore, written to all the umpires on the list of that year, and have received a categorical denial from each umpire that any such instruction or advice was given or implied.'

Throwing, or 'chucking' as it was emotively described, had returned to bedevil cricket's administrators at the end of the 1950s, following the difficulties encountered by Peter May's team in Australia in 1958–59. Ian Meckiff, Jim Burke, Gordon Rorke and Keith Slater, of the Australian Test bowlers, appeared to most English observers to contravene Law 26 as it then was – 'For a delivery to be fair the ball must be bowled, not thrown or jerked' – but none was no-balled during the series. However, as that previously mentioned *Cricketer* comment in June 1965 indicated, English cricket's own house was not in order, and MCC was forced to admit in 1959 that for some time it had had misgivings about the actions of some bowlers in England. Certainly there were plenty of batsmen, English and touring, who were of the opinion that Surrey's left-arm spinner Tony Lock had been throwing them out for years. Now umpires and county officials were instructed to take all necessary steps to rectify the situation.

The interesting thing is that Lock and the other suspect bowlers were allowed by umpires and their own counties to play on regardless of the Laws of the game. It was, I think, Doug Insole who turned to the square-leg umpire when bowled out by Lock and asked if he had been bowled or run out. It's a good story. But is it a laughing matter that first-class cricket, and Test cricket, in England was conducted with the umpires not always applying the Laws? It is true that the umpire had to make a judgement, but he has to make a judgement in the case of lbw appeals and bat-pad catches. The Laws of Cricket are not Draconian measures dreamed up by pedantic administrators to prevent cricketers enjoying themselves. They are there to ensure that batsmen and bowlers compete on as equal terms as possible. It doesn't say much for those who play the game when cricketers, revealing the tendency of human nature to weakness, break or circumvent the Laws; it says just as little about those expected to uphold the Laws when either by omission or commission they allow certain transgressions to pass unchecked. Perhaps they do so in some ill-conceived belief that they are maintaining the spirit of the game rather than the letter of the law, a dubious practice at the best of times. The spirit of the game, after all, is dependent on the letter of the law.

As a defence of English umpires' inaction, or unawareness, when it came to calling throwers, it was often pointed out that no-balling a suspect bowler might bring an end to his playing career. This, it was suggested, would inhibit an umpire when it came to calling transgressors. What about the batsman whose career might have depended on one good innings, only to have it denied him by a bowler with an unfair action? It was not as if there was always an element of doubt either. MCC's admission that they had 'for some time entertained misgivings about the doubtful actions of certain bowlers' discounted that. It came down to one of two things, or a combination of both: weak umpiring in a country whose umpires were flatteringly claimed to be the best in the world, or a conspiracy of 'unawareness' involving players, umpires and administrators.

Certainly the umpires' lot was not made easier by counties who either showed a blinding ignorance of the Laws, or high-handedly hoped they would get away with contravening them. Was there no one at Middlesex, for example, with doubts about the young Dominican fast bowler Pat Lawrence in 1964 — a time when throwing was in everyone's minds? Off a run of some six paces, he was reported to be promisingly sharp, but his first-class career lasted for just four games. In the last of these, against Sussex at Lord's, he was called twice for throwing by umpire Ron Aspinall in his first three overs and did not bowl again.

'It is difficult to follow the reasoning of Middlesex,' Leslie Smith, a senior member of the Cricket Reporting Agency, wrote. 'Surely officials and cricketers must know that a bowler's action is doubtful, especially when the supposedly "non-expert" can see at a glance.' Smith's non-expert was a colleague who had seen the twenty-one-year-old Lawrence at pre-season nets and had returned to Fleet Street 'shaking his head and casting doubts about his action'. When Smith himself made enquiries, he was met by a 'blank silence. Nobody was prepared to commit himself.'

The Middlesex authorities, concluded Smith, 'must take the blame for launching him into first-class cricket under such circumstances. Did they have no suspicion whatsoever? It is hard to imagine that nobody at the ground of the Headquarters of cricket who saw him could not spot a doubtful action. Umpires have a difficult enough job without having the onus thrust on them. Aspinall is to be admired for having the courage of his convictions.'*

Aspinall did not stand in a match played by the West Indians in 1963, but he did umpire several games in which Charlie Griffith played when they returned in 1966. He did not no-ball Griffith for throwing, although by now the big fast bowler's action was under such scrutiny that, by and large, he passed muster. However, as the *Wisden* editor, Norman Preston, commented in his review of the 1966 tour, 'When Griffith attempted his fullest pace, or his bouncer or yorker, he seemed to have to take care and was seldom the same deadly bowler as on his previous visit. At times, Sobers preferred to take the new ball himself.'

Ironically, given the column inches devoted to Griffith's action, the press, although well represented, failed to notice when he was first called in 1966 – by Arthur Fagg in the West Indians' match

* *The Cricketer*, 5 June 1964

against Lancashire at Old Trafford. During the Lancashire innings Griffith was called nine times for over-stepping by Fagg's fellow-umpire, Fred Jakeman, and it was on one of these occasions that Fagg at square leg simultaneously called him for throwing. It was only the second time a member of a touring team in England had been called for throwing,* but it was not until the next morning, when the Lancashire players arrived at Lord's for their Gillette Cup game against Middlesex, that the press came to hear of it. These days, as in the mystery of the replacement ball in the England–Pakistan one-day international at Lord's, they would have been among the first to know. Cricket still had some sense of honour in the 1960s, even if former Test captains such as Ted Dexter and Richie Benaud, not to mention the current Australian captain, Bobby Simpson, were uncompromising in their assessment of Griffith's bowling action. Dexter was still a county player – under similar restraints to Lamb in 1992 – when he delivered his infamous verdict that the result of the 1963 series between England and West Indies was meaningless.

Although photographs illustrated that Charlie Griffith might throw, including some explicit ones used by Benaud to support his argument, E. W. Swanton correctly pointed out that, 'As an indication of the value of stills it may be mentioned that Sir Donald Bradman has a picture library from which it might be "proved" that half the great bowlers of all ages have been throwers.'† Photographs, moreover, could be taken from a variety of angles. The umpire had to decide on a bowler's action from his situation at square leg, some thirty to forty yards away, while the bowler's arm came over at a considerable speed. When the suspect delivery was irregular, as it was in the case of Charlie Griffith, the umpire's job was even harder.

---

* The first was the South African fast bowler Geoff Griffin, who on their 1960 tour of England was no-balled twenty-eight times for throwing in four first-class matches by seven umpires. Unable to straighten his arm properly since an accident as a schoolboy, he quickly became the subject of doubts about the legality of his action, showing many of the symptoms endemic in a thrower. In England in 1960 he was first no-balled at Lord's during the tourists' match against MCC, and subsequently in three other games, the last being the Second Test at Lord's.
† *The Cricketer*, April 1965.

In between plugging steadily away at just over fast-medium, Charlie had the ability to unleash either a mean bouncer or a deadly yorker. Both were genuinely quick and had the knack of either hitting the stumps or the unfortunate recipient, who was usually unable to detect the increase in speed until it was too late. He also possessed a slower ball which was extremely well disguised and difficult to pick. Not surprisingly, many batsmen, among them as good a judge as the late Ken Barrington, maintained that Charlie's ability to produce this sudden extra pace, or the splendid slower ball, came about because he threw those deliveries. True, he had many of the characteristics of a thrower, including the splayed left foot and the early opening up and dropping away of his left shoulder, but I was never able to make up my mind. This despite batting against him on many occasions, and also having him as a member of the West Indian team which I managed for Rothmans during their short tour to England.*

Barrington was so convinced that Griffith threw, indeed had thrown in England in 1963 even though he was never called, that he refused to play for the England XI against the West Indians in those Rothmans fixtures at the back end of the 1964 season. In view of what came to light the following year, he was probably wise to refuse, even if his absence did preclude the delightful prospect of the opened-up batsman facing the opened-up bowler. However, the coaching manual, with its adherence to cricket being a side-on game, was not the only book being thrown out the window. The rule book was also subject to defenestration, as the *Daily Mail* revealed in June 1965 when it published letters said to have been stolen from the briefcase of umpire Cec Pepper. The previous year, his first on the first-class umpires' list, Pepper had umpired at Edgbaston in the second of the three games between An England XI and Sir Frank Worrell's XI, the other two being at Scarborough and Lord's, and this Edgbaston match was the subject of Pepper's letter to MCC which appeared in the *Daily Mail*.

* Trevor Bailey. *From Larwood to Lillee* (Queen Anne Press, 1983)

Prior to the start, Pepper wrote, he was asked by Trevor Bailey 'not to call any bowler, and to be lenient on the front foot rule, as it was exhibition cricket and incidents were, if possible, to be avoided'. Bailey, the Essex captain and secretary, was the manager of the West Indies team and also captain of the England elevens at Scarborough and Lord's. Dexter captained the England XI at Edgbaston. 'I feel, however,' Pepper continued, 'that having stood at square leg for the first time with Charles Griffith of the West Indies bowling, I should draw your attention to the fact that had it been other than an exhibition match, I would have had no hesitation in calling him for throwing.'

In fact, it is incorrect to describe those matches as 'exhibition cricket', for all three fixtures, while friendly games, were none the less accorded first-class status. Incorrect, too, for approaches to be made to an umpire, requesting him to be lenient in his interpretation of the Laws. Certainly cause for concern at Lord's, one would like to think. Yet the reply to Pepper's letter, from Donald Carr, the assistant-secretary of MCC, indicated anything but concern. 'I entirely approve of the steps you have taken in this matter,' he wrote, 'since it would undoubtedly have caused unnecessary unpleasantness if you had "called" him in an exhibition match of this sort.'

It would also have caused unnecessary embarrassment to MCC to have Griffith called for throwing so soon after all their efforts to bring the West Indians back on a full tour of England in 1966, only three years after their financial triumph in 1963. Publicity of the wrong kind would not have been welcomed by the sponsors either, a consideration very much in the mind of sports bodies when it comes to keeping commercial interests happy.

Cricket, part of whose marketing profile is its image as a well-mannered game encapsulating all that is good in English life, can afford to court controversy less than other sports. But the way to do that is to root out and expel the lawbreakers; not to compromise the integrity of the umpires or, as happened at Lord's in 1992, lock away the evidence and act as if nothing has happened.

This serves only to expose the shaky foundations on which the edifice of international and commercial cricket has been built. When the product is given primacy ahead of the law, that is no longer cricket.

16

The Snare of Diplomacy

During the great ball-abuse debate in 1992, a former county wicket-keeper in conversation opined that it was all a fuss about nothing: the ball, he said, should be the bowler's. Batsmen had things too much their own way. Heavier bats reduced the need for skill and favoured brawn ahead of brain; they got away with murder on the lbw law, playing with the bat behind the pad – a stroke that is not a stroke at all because the bat cannot hit the ball if the batsman's leg is deliberately positioned between the two. Old bowlers came and went, telling tricks of the trade as old as the game itself. Fast bowlers, if the stories were believed, spent so much time lifting the seam that it is a wonder they had the strength to bowl at all after their exertions. Umpires seem to have carried penknives in their pockets for no better reason than to offer them to bowlers who chewed their fingernails and so couldn't pick the seam properly – or improperly. Arthur Mailey, in that wonderful autobiography* of his, recounts how he carried pow-dered resin in his pocket, rubbing it into the ball to obtain a better grip – and a better tweak. When the resin ran out – spin bowlers put in long spells in Mailey's day – he made it his business to shake hands frequently with Bert Oldfield, the wicket-keeper's gloves being coated, legitimately, with bird-lime. He was also happy, he tells, to pick the seam for the fast men, Gregory and McDonald, until it was time to rosin up the ball and fiddle out some batsmen.

* *10 for 66 and All That* (Phoenix House, 1958)

Deliberately scuffing one side of the ball, using a fingernail or something less personal, is a more recent phenomenon. Although bowlers have always worked at keeping one side of the ball polished – except in 1966 when as an experiment it was banned for a season – it used to be that natural forces took their toll on the 'unpolished' side. The speed with which the ball lost its shine on the hard Australian grounds of the 1920s and 1930s, quickly removing the possibility of swing at pace, is given as one of the reasons for the use of bodyline bowling in 1932–33. Modern top-dressing, unfortunately, keeps the outfield lush, with the result that the shine stays on the ball longer. Consequently, the contrast of rough and smooth, professed by some exponents to be a component of swing, is longer coming, and that is why some bowlers took matters into their own hands, so to speak. How it works is another matter. The dynamics of swing have always been beyond my comprehension: they sound too much like physics, which in my education was on a par with ball-room dancing. Better to think of swing like seduction. Sometimes it works, sometimes it doesn't. It depends on the environment and the atmosphere; some are better at it than others; some work at it more. Others go through life hoping to bowl the perfect googly.

The real fascination of the ball-tampering scandal was the opportunity it provided to observe English attitudes to foreigners. By making allegations of ball abuse, the press implied that England lost the Test series because the Pakistanis cheated, just as it was the Germans' fault when Britain had to withdraw from the Exchange Rate Mechanism and let the pound freefall. It was much easier to blame someone else for these unpalatable defeats, rather than acknowledge the fact that in 1992 England (or Britain) was not up to it. The trouble with Pakistanis, it seems, is that they are proud and proudly nationalistic, and of all the former countries of the British Empire where cricket is played they are the least English. They have remained foreign, retaining a rich culture that draws on Persia and the Indian sub-continent, and while the foreigner in England may be welcomed, he is rarely understood. The fact that the Pakistanis' cricket, like their temperament, can be

volatile is part of its attraction, for, as long as it remains within
the Laws of the game, that volatility broadens cricket's appeal. If
variety is the spice of life, there is no reason why cricket should
not benefit from a dash of coriander.

Cricket, MCC secretary Griffith said in 1964, 'has, for most
Britishers, a unique image, quite different from any other sport.
Above all, nothing must be done which will damage that image
in any way.' He went on to refer to 'cricket's time-honoured code
of behaviour', but the way other countries have viewed this code,
and cricket's unique image, has not always coincided with that of
some Britishers. Two years earlier, in 1962, the Pakistan team
touring England – complimented in *Wisden* for the way management and players 'met their reverses as sportsmen and were a
popular party wherever they went' – had expressed concern at the
amount of bad language encountered from English players, both
in England and when they had visited Pakistan. Allegations of
gamesmanship included unpleasant remarks being made by English
players to upset the batsman's concentration, and after some incidents captains had to apologize for their players' manners. An
Indian Test cricketer, who played in the Lancashire leagues, once
told Leslie Smith he had been amazed at the words used on the
field. 'Having lived in England for some time, he more or less
became used to it and realised that only rarely was the abuse
intended. "With my broader outlook, I was able to answer
them back in the same way," he said. "Unfortunately, most of the
Indian players are upset when it happens and take it as a personal insult."'* It is not possible to say whether or not such
behaviour was part of the time-honoured code, if only because
one of my predecessors as editor of *Wisden* once mentioned by
name senior amateur cricketers as being amongst the foremost
exponents of sledging in English cricket. One of them was a
county captain.

When, early on that 1962 tour, the Pakistanis paid their first
visit to Lord's for the traditional match against MCC, their opponents were captained by Donald Carr, captain of Derbyshire and

* *The Cricketer*, 21 July 1962

then in his final season before becoming assistant-secretary
of MCC. He was not, incidentally, one of the aforementioned
sledgers. Carr's appointment to captain MCC against the tourists
is noteworthy because, in the winter of 1955–56, he had captained
to Pakistan an MCC A side that found itself at the centre of a
blaze of controversy. What had begun as a joke – to the tourists
if not to their hosts – threatened to backfire into a diplomatic
incident of sufficient seriousness for the president of MCC, Lord
Alexander of Tunis, to offer to bring the MCC team home if it
would help restore friendly relations between MCC and Pakistan.
In addition, he was prepared to compensate the Board of Control
for Cricket in Pakistan (BCCP) for any financial loss arising from
the tour ending prematurely.

As in the best controversies there are two versions of what
happened: the English version and the Pakistani version. Common
to both, though, is that Idries Begh, a Pakistani umpire, had two
buckets of water thrown over him by MCC players at Dean's
Hotel, Peshawar, on the third night of the third representative
match between Pakistan and MCC. In dispute is whether or not
he was a willing party to the escapade by his presence at the
team's hotel. Either he arrived there of his own volition or at the
'insistence' of certain English players. In addition to umpiring in
the game in progress – Pakistan with eight wickets in hand were
eight runs from their second win of the series – Idries Begh had
stood in the two previous representative games, even though Carr
had written to the Pakistan Board after the first representative
match, complaining of Begh's umpiring. If the England players
were surprised to find Idries Begh appointed for the second game,
his presence at Peshawar for the third was confirmation, were
confirmation needed, that things were done differently in Pakistan
from at home. Someone decided that the time had come for Idries
Begh to get his come-uppance by way of the 'water treatment';
the consequence, depending on the version, was that the umpire
lost face or was insulted. The episode was reported to the Pakistan
Board and the MCC players were carpeted. The team manager,
Geoffrey Howard, later claimed that the ragging of the umpire
had no connection with his decisions in the three games, but this

leaves one feeling that the only person missing on the scene was Mandy Rice-Davies.*

The MCC committee, conducting an inquest into the affair, found that Carr, as captain, 'should have recognised at once that this "ragging", although initiated by nothing more than high spirits and with no harmful intent whatsoever, might be regarded, as it was in many quarters, as an attack upon an umpire. The committee are satisfied that this was not the case. The committee consider that the responsibility for the incident rests entirely with the captain and he has been so informed.' The day after that reprimand Carr accepted full responsibility; six years later he was leading MCC at Lord's against the Pakistanis. I don't suppose anyone at MCC gave it a second thought that Carr's appointment might touch a sensitive Pakistani nerve. And they could be sure that the Pakistanis, captained by the Oxford Blue Javed Burki and managed by the courteous Brigadier R. G. Hyder, would not make the kind of fuss the South Africans made two years earlier when they demanded the removal of umpire Buller from the Test panel after he no-balled Geoff Griffin at Lord's. Besides, wicket-keeper Imtiaz Ahmed remembered how promptly Carr had acted in the fourth representative match, at Karachi, when he objected to some of the MCC close-in fielders 'using words among themselves which upset him while he was preparing to take strike'.† These days, the complaints as often as not come from English players, but when they object to the language used by some Pakistani players they should keep in mind that English is not the Pakistanis' first language. What they have learned in English was learned initially from Englishmen.

Unfortunately perhaps for simple cricketers, the relationship between England and Pakistan has a significance beyond the playing of cricket, and this has been a catalyst for conflict and

---

* At the trial of Stephen Ward in 1963 which followed the so-called Profumo affair, Mandy Rice-Davies was asked by counsel if she was aware that Lord Astor had made a statement to the police saying that her allegations were absolutely untrue. Miss Rice-Davies's reply, 'He would, wouldn't he,' was greeted with appreciable and appreciative laughter.
† Joint statement issued by D. B. Carr, the MCC captain, and Fazal Mahmood, the acting Pakistan captain, on 12 March 1956

confusion, particularly among those in England who see cricket as a world enclosed within its own demesne. For those who protest that politics and sport should not mix or be mixed, it must be doubly difficult to accept that cricket, when it involves England and Pakistan, is an ingredient of international politics; an ingredient, moreover, which appears to English eyes to favour Pakistan. But to a British Foreign Office that sees world affairs as they pertain to Foreign Office policy as much (if not more than) they pertain to Britain, Pakistan is strategically and diplomatically important as a former Commonwealth country bordering on Iran, Afghanistan, China and India, with the former Soviet Union to the north. Cricket is a means of maintaining links, which is why in cricketing disputes between the two countries England will always be seen to come off second best. Something more important than cricket is involved, which is why Allan Lamb, South African born and bred to see issues in black and white, did not just break the rules when he went to the *Daily Mirror* with his 'cheating' exposure. He overturned a season of diplomatic endeavour to ensure that Anglo-Pakistan relations – beyond the boundary – were not strained.

For English cricketers playing in Pakistan, the frustrations of touring are exaggerated by alien conditions and culture. 'Face', as in the case of the watered-down umpire, Idries Begh, is an element to be considered in every transaction; so is patience, a quality in shorter supply in modern Western life than in the East. One has only to watch Americans at breakfast in Spain to appreciate the demands on restraint expected of an English cricketer outside his own environment. In this respect, the Test and County Cricket Board's responsibility towards the teams it sends to Pakistan must extend beyond mere playing preparations. Managers, captain and players require an awareness, not only of what might confront them there but of what is expected of them. The real tragedy of Mike Gatting's verbal brawl with umpire Shakoor Rana at Faisalabad in December 1987 – 'two grown men standing on their dignity without a square inch of moral ground to support them'*

---

* *Wisden Cricketers' Almanack 1988*

– was that the England captain felt he had been betrayed by the insistence that he back down. The betrayal was in not making him aware, when he was appointed to take the team to Pakistan, that he could never come off anything but second best. This should have been a condition of acceptance. The enmity that surfaced on the field and in the press on Pakistan's tour of England earlier in the year had provided every indication needed that England's tour of Pakistan could be fraught with frustration for the England party. If nothing else, the TCCB should have been aware of the dangers ahead. Every precaution to avoid them should have been taken.

The precedent for cricket taking second place to diplomacy when England meet Pakistan is the MCC tour of Ceylon and Pakistan in 1968–69, arranged to fill the void left by the cancellation of MCC's tour of South Africa. A country of diverse population groups, divided by race and extremes of wealth and poverty, Pakistan was also divided geographically into West and East Pakistan. The latter has been a separate country, Bangladesh, since 1971 but at the time of the visit by MCC, East and West Pakistan were riven by regional dissent, rioting and all the bloodier acolytes of civil disorder. It was no place for a cricket tour, and there was every reason, from the point of view of cricketers, why the team should not have gone there in the first place. Such was the extent of the disturbances that the East Pakistan section of the tour was initially cancelled while the MCC team were still comfortably harboured in Ceylon. That England eventually played a Test match in Dacca, the capital of East Pakistan, illustrates the confusion and political manoeuvring MCC encountered once they arrived in Pakistan.

On landing in Karachi, having flown from Colombo, the team were told by the secretary of the Pakistan Board that they would fly on to Bahawalpur at six o'clock the next morning. It was not what they expected; it was not what they needed. Also present at this meeting, Michael Melford reported in *The Cricketer*, 'were the Deputy British High Commissioner and the High Commissioner's military adviser. They gave valuable advice and help but not even the High Commissioner himself, then in Rawalpindi, would at any time give captain [Colin Cowdrey] and manager [Les Ames] a firm directive.' E. M. Wellings' report in *Wisden* was decidedly less diplomatic. 'Again cricket became a pawn in an unsavoury political game . . . That it [the tour] was kept going from crisis to crisis was due to the ruling politicians of Pakistan and the diplomats of Britain. They seemed anxious for the cricket to be played regardless of the safety of the players. If they hoped the games would exert a calming influence, their calculations were sadly awry. The Test matches rather served as rallying points for the agitators.' Ames, Wellings went on to say, praising the manager for his calmness throughout, 'received worthless assurances from Pakistan officials and misleading advice and information from British sources'. In spite of this he somehow 'steered the team through the chaotic difficulties of this ill-starred venture'. Another British journalist, Alex Bannister of the *Daily Mail*, said that 'the local Board and British diplomats shirked the responsibility of calling a halt to the wretched and dangerous situation. Cricket was used as a political shuttlecock.'* It still is, and is still allowed to be. It was no more possible for Gatting's team to end their tour prematurely in 1987 than it had been for Cowdrey's to get away from riot-torn Pakistan in 1969. It took a mob storming the National Stadium at Karachi on the third day of the Third Test to bring home to the Pakistan authorities the futility of trying to play cricket, and at last a tour which should never have begun was abandoned.

For Cowdrey it was an unhappy end to what was to be his last tour and series as England's captain. His Achilles tendon injury in May kept him out of the 1969 Tests and let in Illingworth. Worse, the abandoned Karachi Test proved to be Colin Milburn's last, for within weeks of returning to England he lost his left eye in a car accident near Northampton. Milburn's larger-than-life presence had been a salve to the beleaguered team when he arrived at Dacca as a reinforcement from Western Australia, where he had been playing in the Sheffield Shield. His hundred off 163 balls on the opening day at Karachi was as great a tonic as his sub-

* *Wisden Cricketers' Almanack 1980*

sequent injury was a loss. Knott deserved all the sympathy he
received for being evacuated with his maiden Test hundred in
sight, but history shows that the seventies were stretched out gloriously ahead of him. For Milburn there were only the memories
of a Test career lasting less than three years, in which the appreciation of the cricketing public was unmatched by his Test
appearances.

The tour also revealed a side of Cowdrey's personality out of
keeping with his public persona. Blessed with an easy charm and
a cautious tact, he had always been the ideal diplomat on tour.
The troubled waters in Pakistan cast him adrift, leaving him uncertain of his bearings. His autobiography tells of his shyness as a
child; the impression is given of an immensely talented schoolboy
cricketer unsure of his place in the social caste of prep and public
school life. One feels in him a desperate longing to be loved by
everyone, combined with a desire to know and be liked by the
right people. The bewildering situation that prevailed in Pakistan
required more than tact or charm, however. It called for a determination inherent in which was the risk, although earning respect, of
not being liked. It was not, necessarily, a situation for a diplomat.

Like Sir Pelham Warner, like Sir George Allen, Sir Colin
Cowdrey made cricket his life. But unlike them, he had to find a
role to fill as cricket spread on to an international field. Whereas
for Warner and Allen cricket was an English game, played to
English traditions in lands governed according to English ways,
Cowdrey saw cricket become a game of national aspirations subject in some countries to national politics. The old paternalism of
the Marylebone Cricket Club no longer sufficed as a sometimes
gentle, sometimes authoritative hand on the tiller, if for no other
reason than it had sold the boat.

Having played a hand in ensuring MCC's acquiescence to the
desires of the TCCB, Cowdrey had at the same time deprived
himself of the power-base that sustained Warner and Allen. He
was not a businessman like the power players at the TCCB, and
though he sat on a number of influential committees at Canterbury
and Lord's he was not drawn to the prolonged conflict of wills
that carried Allen triumphantly through interminable hours of

committee-room debate. His strength lay outside the committee-room, where the full force of his personality was brought into play. A public person to the world at large, he none the less had a diplomat's feel for the reserved conversations behind closed doors.

So with all roads no longer leading to Lord's, he went on the road. Some years, it seemed, only the Grateful Dead and the Foreign Secretary spent more time away from home. As president of MCC, Cowdrey had also been chairman of the ICC,* an aged and toothless body that for most of its life had celebrated its existence by meeting annually at Lord's. For a long time it was considered so irrelevant that not all countries bothered sending a delegate from home, preferring to be represented by a proxy in England who had no authority to do anything without referring back to the national governing body. MCC ran the ICC with a customary efficiency, and no doubt the system was very much to their liking. Once in a while, even, the member countries would agree to a compromise and the secretary could emerge waving a piece of paper.

Three things precipitated a major change in the way the ICC operated: money, national interests and the 747. The advance in international travel accelerated by long-haul jet aircraft made it easier for the officials of the different governing bodies to visit Lord's themselves for the annual meeting in mid-summer. The prospect of a financial windfall from the mooted World Cup competitions, and later the threat exposed by Kerry Packer's World Series Cricket to what had seemed a comfortable club, provided them with the incentive to meet regularly and protect their own interests. There was also, for some countries, a requirement to observe their governments' policies towards South Africa and keep that country outside the framework of international cricket.

---

* Founded in 1909 as the Imperial Cricket Conference by Australia, England and South Africa, the ICC was initially confined to the governing bodies of cricket in countries within the British Commonwealth where Test cricket was played. Consequently, when South Africa left the Commonwealth in 1961 it ceased to be a member of the ICC. By the time Pakistan left the Commonwealth in 1971, however, the rules had been revised, in 1965, to include countries from outside the Commonwealth, and the Conference had been renamed the International Cricket Conference. It became the International Cricket Council in 1989.

In addition, the club expanded. At the 1962 meeting of the ICC, Pakistan proposed the formation of a 'junior section', the general idea being that the Test-playing countries should take the minor cricket-playing countries under their wing on some zonal basis. Two years later it was proposed that future membership should be open to any country where cricket was 'firmly established and organized', and in 1965 Ceylon, Fiji and the United States were invited to join as Associate Members. Since then the Associates have swelled to the extent that, while having only one vote to the Full Members' two, they outnumber the Test-playing countries as a voting block. This has given the Associates an importance in cricket's international administration beyond anything most members would have contemplated when their introduction was first raised by Pakistan in the early 1960s.

Although its decisions were a long time coming, and often couched in laborious language, the ICC was becoming a potential international commission for cricket by the time it was renamed the International Cricket Council in 1989, and revised rules were adopted. This followed three years of meetings, under the chairmanship of Raman Subba Row, a former chairman of the TCCB, which examined the machinery, role and method of the ICC's operation. In fact, the revised ICC could have been tailor-made for Subba Row's friend Colin Cowdrey, for it gave him a new role in cricket. Under the new structure, the chairmanship of the ICC ceased being the concurrent office of the president of MCC and became a four-year appointment, nominated by the president of MCC and approved by ICC members. In 1989, Field-Marshal The Lord Bramall nominated Cowdrey, the member countries approved, and from October he became the Henry Kissinger of cricket, embarking on a diplomatic shuttle to solve the game's problems.

Four years later, and now Sir Colin Cowdrey, he could look back on some considerable achievements. South Africa had been readmitted to the international fold – and through Cowdrey's efforts the South Africans competed in the 1992 World Cup in Australia and New Zealand within months of their return. A Code of Conduct was introduced to deal with such contentious issues as sledging, short-pitched bowling and dissent by players at umpires' decisions. The principle of match referees, to back up umpires and to impose penalties, had been accepted and brought into practice. Despite criticism that it was too little too late, and that the ICC remained little more than a toothless tiger, Cowdrey had in fact done much to bring cricket into repute at a time when there seemed no shortage of candidates ready to do the opposite.

What Cowdrey's role as roving ambassador illustrated was the way an international body could function, given finance and organization. The first steps towards a truly administrative ICC came in 1993 with the appointment of ICC's first chief executive, David Richards, formerly the chief executive of the Australian Cricket Board. The extent to which the position allowed its incumbent to be servant or master was untested, but the possibilities were there for the chief executive of the ICC to be cricket's answer to Jacques Delors.* A chief executive with vision and ambition could write an agenda for international cricket which would strengthen ICC's administration while the member countries became secondary to it, rather as the centralized Test and County Cricket Board grew in importance at the counties' expense.

The other issue, albeit speculative, is how long it will be before that administrative base switches from West to East; from London to, say, Lahore. Despite their political animosity, India and Pakistan were able to join forces to stage the 1987 World Cup and to win the bid for the 1995 World Cup, which England initially expected to hold on the basis of rotation. For their 1995 bid India and Pakistan were joined by Sri Lanka, and a prominent feature of their proposal was its financial incentives to the Associate Members, whose support could have been crucial in determining the venue. When the Full Members could not reach the required two-thirds majority among themselves, however, England eventually withdrew their bid at the end of a day-long meeting described by the chief executive of the TCCB as 'fractious and unpleasant . . . It was beset by procedural wrangling and there was no talk of anything like cricket.'

---

* President of the European Commission 1985–

It will be only a matter of time before a representative from either India or Pakistan is nominated as chairman of the ICC; there will be those in both countries ambitious to have cricket's international offices located there. South Africa, too, has a case, being well situated geographically for many member countries, and in losing its traditional role as the headquarters of cricket, Lord's will in turn cease to be seen as the spiritual centre of the game. But how will cricket's supporters in England react when the game, *their* game as many have thought of it for generations, is subject to changes emanating from abroad? During the furore that followed Gatting's spat with Shakoor Rana, and vice versa, Ray Illingworth, as astute an observer of cricket's affairs as he was a captain, expressed his fear that the prolonged dispute was 'an international plot to deprive this country [England] of its influence in world cricket – a political power game'. Whether there was a conspiracy or not, he was right in one respect. In relation to its place in world affairs when Illingworth made his debut for Yorkshire in 1951, England has lost its over-riding influence in world cricket. It will always be the game's senior player, but the days have gone when an English *eminence grise* such as Gubby Allen could cross the world pulling strings. Encouraged by Raman Subba Row's ICC sub-committee in the late 1980s, and shown the way by Sir Colin Cowdrey's diplomatic chairmanship of the Council from 1989 to 1993, cricket has passed into the hands of the international community.

17

Conclusions on the Wall

Did you ever expect a corporation to have a conscience, when it has no soul to be damned, and no body to be kicked?

Lord Thurlow, 1731–1806

When I resigned as editor of *Wisden Cricketers' Almanack* in April 1992, it was partly because I was disillusioned with the way cricket was going. It was also so that I would have time to think and write. This, however, was not the book I had thought of writing, even if I did prompt its conception by something I wrote in the 1992 *Wisden*. It is not a cricket history. All I set out to do was stimulate thought and in the process, perhaps, entertain.

What I wrote in the 1992 *Wisden* described the difference of opinion between the Cricket and Marketing committees of the Test and County Cricket Board as illustrating 'the struggle for the soul of the game'. It is a fine-sounding phrase, equally useful for describing conflicts within the Church of England, the Conservative Party, the Labour Party and other such establishment bodies. Useful, too, when asking which road Britain is going down. The problem with using a word like soul, though, is that it requires some definition, even if everyone thinks he or she knows what you mean. Soul is especially troublesome in a secular society because it is redolent of religion and philosophy: simpler to go along with the definition of Epictetus according to Stephen Dedalus. The soul is very like a bucketful of water.* Had Donald Carr been sufficiently quick-witted, he could have explained away the 1956 Peshawar water incident as an attempt to show umpire Idries Begh what was meant by the soul of cricket.

There is also the not-insignificant matter of what is meant by cricket. For me it is a game anyone can play: men and women, boys and girls, plus the family dog as a fielder when appropriate. I enjoy watching a bowler bowl and a batsman bat, whether on a forecourt in a lunch break, at a public park or at a county ground. The pleasure increases with the standard of play, but at heart the game remains the same. It belongs to anyone who wants to play it, watch it, keep the score or assemble minefields of statistics. If cricket has a soul, it is this accessibility to all who enjoy being part of it. It can exist on its own without organization, without a body. Just as a church is its people, not its buildings or its rituals – 'Where two or three are gathered together in My name' – so cricket can exist without Lord's, MCC, the TCCB and the ICC.

When I wrote 'the struggle for the soul of the game', however, I was not thinking of cricket in a catholic sense. My concern was for first-class cricket in England; for the county game; for the cricket which has given the sport such a special place in English life. It has provided a focus of association for all cricket-lovers. It has created heroes who live on in old men's memories from those days when as boys they stretched along the boundary with their sandwiches and autograph books. These days, old men and boys have to sit behind the boundaries lest they conceal the advertisements. Yet it was not so long ago, certainly well into the 1970s, when several thousand spectators could sit on the grass at Lord's on Test match days. I did so myself. But marketing took priority over men and boys and girls with picnic baskets, and those days are just another cricket memory.

Time alone will tell how many boys of today will be old men with memories of cricketers tomorrow. Not only boys, either. We all need the Gowers and Bothams, the Gattings and

---

* James Joyce. *Portrait of the Artist as a Young Man* (Jonathan Cape, 1916)

Gooches, the Waqars and Wasims to do what in our private worlds we would hardly dare do. We need them to elevate us. And we also need the honest journeymen whom John Arlott so loved because with his poet's eye he recognized and understood the honesty with which they gave their all to cricket. They give us hope that there, with practice, patience and some good fortune, we could go, treading the same fields as the gods. In their own way they are as important heroes as the gods, for they too feed the nostalgia and the fantasies on which the county game has been sustained through generations. But for how much longer?

It is that same county game, which has survived and nurtured generations, that I see as the soul of cricket: cricket at the top level as it belongs to the people. The body within which this soul resides is the Test and County Cricket Board – and many may agree with those Greeks who thought it is only when the soul leaves the body that it can show its true nature. What concerns me is this particular soul's ability to live outside the body. That, I feel, has been the essence of the struggle since the counties took on the responsibility for fully professional cricketers and set themselves up as a business. The counties have lost their independence, in that they can no longer exist without the TCCB, whose business plan is the promotion of cricket through the England team.

There is a good logic to the Board's strategy. As spectators, the English love grand sporting occasions: many who never attend a county game will go to a Test match or watch it on television. From my own experience, requests for tickets to a Lord's cup final come from those who have never been to an earlier round of the competition. Similarly, an attempt to stage a play-off tournament among the top four of the Sunday League never caught on because the final lacked the sense of occasion that goes with a Lord's final. (It would be interesting to see if the same crowds would be drawn if the All-England Club held its tennis championships in Nottingham, say, instead of at Wimbledon, with all the tradition and swank associated with its annual fortnight.) From the business viewpoint, major sponsorships and television rights are better sold as a national package, leaving the individual counties to deal with local sponsors and advertisers.

What would happen if there ceased to be the same *raison d'être* for the England team? With the reform of the County Championship from three-day cricket to four-day games, the traditional format of an English season has been changed radically to accommodate both the technical and logistical demands of the national squad, as the England team is in all but name. The politically correct fellow in the woodpile in this, however, is the decline in attendances at Test matches in many of the Test-playing countries.

How many years are left for Test cricket if crowds continue to decline, as they do in countries other than England? The return of South Africa to the international fold presents both an opportunity and a challenge. The opportunity lies in a population deprived of international cricket for twenty years. The challenge will be in sustaining an audience for Test cricket after the initial enthusiasm is satisfied. The new generation, unaccustomed to the gradual development of a Test match, may wonder what all the fuss was about. A one-day international under lights, on a warm evening flavoured by steaks cooking on a barbecue, may well be what they want. Cricket currently needs the variety that South Africa will bring, but as the new South Africans seek their place in the sun, they could also quicken the erosion of what one increasingly thinks of as traditional cricket.

When I wrote that in the 1992 *Wisden* I did think there would be a better response to Test cricket in South Africa than there was for their first comeback series, against India in 1992–93. A series against West Indies, Australia or England would have been a truer guide to the standing of Test cricket in the republic, but it was an ominous portent that the one-day internationals between South Africa and India were constantly well supported.

If countries other than England decide there is no future in Test cricket, the next stage will be their deciding that there is no need to maintain an unwatched first-class game that consumes time and money – both valuable commodities in countries where the game is not fully professional. Competitive club competitions would continue to bring players to the top for national and international one-day tournaments, as they had previously done for the first-class game in these countries, but the grounding for Test cricket, the first-class game, would have been lost. In time, and not a long time at that, countries would no longer want to send Test teams to England. They would not have sufficient experience: they would rather play one-day games against the counties and a series of, say, five one-day internationals against England. Where then would be the need for the four-day Championship game that few county members wanted?

The next question, then, concerns the future of first-class county cricket if there is no Test cricket for the England team on which the marketing of cricket is structured. More to the point, was this ever considered when the marketing strategy was devised, at a time when the overseas market looked at best short term and at worst terminal? Although it is not always obvious at ground level, there is still sufficient interest and belief in first-class cricket to sustain a county circuit, but not on the heavily subsidized scale that has snowballed, providing for big squads of retained players and generous administrative staffs. Cricket-lovers will always support their counties to the best of their ability, provided they feel comfortable with the game. This has been the tradition of county cricket. Today, however, many of those loyal supporters fear that traditions have been set aside for a brave new world in which they are second-class citizens. Furthermore they feel there is a danger that the Test and County Cricket Board is gambling with county cricket's future as well as its past. All the Board's sponsorships, which along with Test cricket make up the essential funding to the counties, are short term. If sponsors can no longer afford to buy cricket, which is after all the TCCB's only product, or no longer want to buy it because the product has changed, the county game as it has become will go out of business.

This is not the same as saying that county cricket will die. It may have to return to being a game more in its own right, as it was before Test cricket became the end which justified the means.

More to the point it may have to be less dependent on money, and consequently less dependent on large staffs: a game with fewer matches so as to provide a concentrated attraction for members and occasional spectators. A game, moreover, in which part-time cricketers can participate. I am not one for praising past times; I prefer to see the past as a signpost to the present. The important issue is the state of the present, and where the present is leading. The past, however, cannot be discounted; it provides us with the only lessons we have.

In the same way that MCC attracted criticism and some unworthy abuse because it was perceived to be the agency of all things wrong with cricket, so the TCCB has become an easy target for those who find the modern game wanting. I have let loose the occasional arrow myself, and drawn the odd head above the sandbags to return fire or cry foul. It may seem a contradiction, in the light of what has gone before, but the Board's administration has generally carried out its duties extremely well. Cricket remains the national summer game; remains in fact the national game when one considers the media coverage the England team receives when on winter tours. International matches are well attended, and through advance bookings, sponsorships and broadcasting fees they bring into the game a wealth beyond imagination when the first sponsored competition was introduced in 1963. Cricket has become an occupation that, with improved wages, attracts most of the best players to the game, while through the National Cricket Association an integrated effort has been made to stream the best schoolboys towards the counties. None of this happened by chance. It could happen only because cricket was skilfully and successfully marketed so that ultimately money could be fed back into the counties and the satellite organizations. The game had to be sold – and for county members struggling or unable to come to terms with the way cricket has been centralized, the writing was on the wall as long ago as the mid-sixties. Actually, it was in *The Cricketer* in May 1967.

Outlining the advisory rôle he had undertaken for MCC and the counties, on cricket's needs in the field of public relations, Denis Morris, recently the Controller of the BBC Light Programme, wrote with some percipience: '. . . I am certain that within a year or two enough money could be raised to provide a working revenue which will allow for considerably improved amenities and higher salaries to players, secretariats and permanent staff, though I suspect that this cannot be achieved without some slight abnegation of individual county autonomy.' Strike out two words, 'some slight', and Morris's statement accurately describes the way cricket is today.

It could have been different had the first-class counties not savagely rejected the Clark Report's main recommendations in 1967.* The players, it is worth pointing out, were emphatically in favour of the structure finally recommended by the report. Only time would tell, Charles Bray reflected in the 1967 *Wisden*, whether or not the counties had signed their own death warrant. And time has shown that they did not. On the other hand they may unwittingly have signed the death warrant of the county cricket they voted not to change. Uncovered pitches, the nursery for ages of English cricketers, the stage on which legendary dramas unfolded, have passed into cricket lore. The three-day game, betrayed by work-to-rule cricketers, remains on death row, awaiting a reprieve from the appeal court or the ministrations of the executioner.

The Clark Report, viewed as history, was the signpost that county cricket ignored as much out of avoidance as ignorance. Throughout the writing of this book, I have gone back to it, finding its defeat as relevant to the struggle for cricket's soul as that 1963 decision to abolish the amateur/professional distinction. That I have not referred to it in detail stems in part from a wish to present an overview, rather than a detailed analysis, of thirty years of cricket, and in part from a knowledge of how quickly some cricket supporters' eyes glaze when confronted with too many technical details. Cricket can be as technical as acting or writing or film-making, but you don't have to know anything about the technique to enjoy any of them. Technical it may have been in some respects, but nevertheless the Clark Report was a brave, intelligent attempt to come to terms with the problems confronting cricket at the

* See page 61

time. It was no fly-by-night affair to cover over cracks or offer solace.

The Clark Committee, bringing together a combination of playing, business and administrative experience, met a number of times from September 1965 to January 1967.* It sent questionnaires to the first-class counties, to county members and to all capped players; rightly convinced that sub-standard pitches produced substandard cricket, it held a conference of all county groundsmen to gather evidence and opinions; it requested the *Daily Mail* to commission a national survey 'to investigate the reasons for the fall in crowds at county grounds and in particular to find out how far the causes of it may be (*a*) counter attractions and present national social habits and (*b*) a feeling that there are defects in the game as a spectator sport on account of the way in which it is played or organised'. Dull and unattractive was the survey's general consensus on county cricket, mainly because of the negative approach of the players.

Even so the committee found that interest in cricket was as great as ever, with the game being played by 'a vast number of people'. There was substantial support from the general public for more one-day cricket, and if enthusiasm for this was more muted among county members, this reflected their love and understanding of the traditional game rather than their rejection of the limited-overs format. These considerations and many others were taken into account in the final recommendations in an attempt to

(*a*) get a more positive and enthusiastic approach by the players,
(*b*) produce a structure that would cause a revival of public interest,

---

* The Clark Committee comprised the following, many of whom have featured in the previous pages: David Clark, chairman and former captain of Kent; Gubby Allen, treasurer of MCC and former captain of England; Charles Bray, former Essex cricketer and veteran cricket correspondent of the *Daily Herald*; Ted Dexter, former captain of England and Sussex; Geoffrey Howard, secretary of Surrey and former secretary of Lancashire; Doug Insole, vice-chairman and former captain of Essex, and chairman of the England Test selectors; Edmund King, chairman of Warwickshire; Brian Sellers, chairman and former captain of Yorkshire; Stuart Surridge, chairman and former captain of Surrey; Fred Titmus, captain of Middlesex; Ken Turner, secretary of Northamptonshire; Mike Turner, secretary of Leicestershire; Ossie Wheatley, captain of Glamorgan.

(*c*) find ways and means of attracting more players into county cricket. In other words to establish a pyramid by which the budding first-class player could graduate from club to county without having to make first-class cricket his sole occupation, as he must do under existing conditions.*

The background to the report was the decline of attendances since the halcyon summers which followed the end of the Second World War.

In 1950 close on 2,000,000 people paid to see Championship cricket in this country. In 1966 the figure had dropped to 513,578. In the early fifties the decline was steady but not unduly alarming. Then the tempo increased at an alarming rate until in recent years it became positively frightening. Worse still was the abrupt halt in the overall increase in [county] membership. In 1964 members totalled 141,707. In 1965 139,964 and in 1966 135,045. To combat the double drop in revenue, counties were compelled to increase subscriptions, which in itself caused a drop in membership.

It was then obvious to all, except those with their heads firmly buried in the sand, that first-class cricket in this country was only solvent because of the efforts of supporters' clubs with football pools and Test match profits.†

Well, we still have Test match profits, plus those from one-day internationals, and sponsorships have reduced the need to rely on the once-vital football pools. But there remains the fact that county cricket is no more able to support itself now than it was in 1967, when committee member Bray concluded that 'A failure of football pools, and most counties would be bankrupt.'

Finding itself responsible for a caravan that had doggedly decided to go round in circles in the middle of a desert, the TCCB has worked miracles to replace its camels with cars (albeit sponsored) and build a four-lane highway on which county cricket can drive farther and farther from its roots. The fear is that, in its

* *Wisden Cricketers' Almanack 1967*
† Ibid.

need to bring in money, it will not know where to stop. Meanwhile, what of MCC, the august club that controlled English cricket for almost 200 years? Where is *it* going? As in the case of the counties, that should be a question for the members; for having in the past left it to their committee to address, gradually more and more of them are coming to the conclusion that the question is being wrongly addressed. Outdistanced by the sponsored cars, the members find that MCC has been left holding the camels.

The Marylebone Cricket Club was uniquely English in that, as a club, it ran a national institution; i.e., cricket. And in its time this worked. The Test and County Cricket Board, on the other hand, has become embracingly international; the national game is controlled by a corporate body as in every country. This too works, in its way, but it is not uniquely English and probably cannot be. Whereas MCC, until its twilight hours of influence, was able to apply pressure internationally, the TCCB has had to bend to international pressures.

The time has now come for MCC to reassess its role in English cricket, for it can still have one, other than being a long stop on the heritage trail. This has, I suspect, to be a role outside the TCCB, and for this to happen the members will have to determine a new direction for the club. Their committee, however experienced and honourable, contains too many who enjoy cross-dressing in MCC tie and TCCB sweatshirt, whereas MCC no longer has a real place in the TCCB. Indeed, it appears to have lost its role in the ICC, bringing home the warning which finished my Editor's Notes in the 1989 *Wisden*. 'In international matters, MCC through the ICC is able to offer counsel which extends beyond parochial issues. Were it ever to content itself simply with its own affairs, MCC would be little more than a cricket club with a Long Room, a long tradition and a long waiting-list.'

Though criticized in the past for being paternalist and feudalist, MCC could just as easily be accused of not interfering enough; especially of allowing the counties too much autonomy in the fifties and sixties as they stumbled in search of solutions, unable to let go of the past, comprehend the present or look to the future. The counties may have been in the hands of men who loved the game and thought they were doing their best for it. But they were without vision, and cricket at that time needed vision. Responsible for the Laws of Cricket, MCC saw itself rather as the conscience of cricket, and if its membership is up to the task, that is the role that cricket needs of the Marylebone Cricket Club today. It is time for the members to stand up and show they belong to MCC for reasons other than easy access to the major games at Lord's and the right to wear the famous 'bacon and egg' tie.

In addition to its internationally known name and its wonderful tradition, MCC has a great asset in Lord's Cricket Ground, and another potentially important one in the wide range of cricketers within its membership. It also has wealthy and influential patrons, as opposed to the TCCB which has sponsors. For many years, MCC has sent sides to play schools XIs, mostly the public schools but not always, in order to preach the gospel of the true cricket at home. Missionary teams have travelled to far-away lands to spread the word, be it or be it not always good news. Now the old faith is under threat at home, and if it is to be defended anywhere, that place must surely be Lord's, the cathedral of English cricket, even if it means breaking away from the established church that has become the Test and County Cricket Board.

Perhaps it needs reiterating that the TCCB does not own cricket in England; it is responsible only for the professional game and for the Test and touring teams that emanate from that game. How it views its responsibility is another matter, and among many for whom cricket is more than a game, that is a matter of grave concern. People are influenced by what they see, and because of television people see so much today. Consequently they are open to many influences, and the young in particular respond to them. 'One sees evidence of this even in the prep schools: I have seen helmets, thigh-pads, warm-up exercises and sweatbands,' wrote a prep-school headmaster in response to an article by John Woodcock, advising the young against 'taking themselves more seriously than they already do'. 'When a mind is impressionable,' wrote Seneca to his friend, Lucilius, 'and has only a shaky hold on what is right, it must be protected from the crowd. It is too easy to follow the majority.' The obvious question presents itself immediately: how long before young cricketers turn out in TCCB-marketed coloured clothing?

As is probably apparent from earlier chapters, I admire the way Micky Stewart and Graham Gooch restored a sense of pride in the England team. Just because their methods met with some success, though, it does not follow that theirs is the only approach to cricket. The game has to be enjoyable, it has to be fun, if cricketers are to be encouraged to play it and to go on playing it for clubs, villages, old boys sides, pubs and whomever, as cricket has always been played in England. This is the heart of cricket, and excessive exercise is not always good for the heart.

That is why the time may be coming for MCC to stage its own matches at Lord's: to show that there is more to cricket than the game promoted by the TCCB. One major match a year would be enough; the Bicentenary match in 1987 showed how well MCC can rise to the occasion. Marching bands and parachutists entertained the shirt-sleeved crowds in the August sun. Gatting, the pugilist, and Gavaskar, the dancing master, set their stall to celebrate 200 years of MCC with double-hundreds, only to fall short at 179 and 188 respectively, and Imran Khan drove Emburey's off-spin high into the President's Box. There was leg-spin from Qadir and left-arm spin from Shastri; Hadlee and Marshall mixed seam, swing and speed in an exhibition of the fast men's art; Greenidge went away with a second-innings century. It was a splendid affair; a match made for the occasion. And August is ideal for such a match at Lord's: the schools are on holiday, the weather is generally favourable, and players from just about every cricket-playing country are available. Such a match, moreover, could offer an opportunity for the highly qualified cricketers outside the county network to pit their skills against some of the world's finest. Given such a perfect setting and a sense of occasion, an exclusively MCC fixture would quickly become as much a tradition as the Lord's Test.

Ah, the Lord's Test. There's the rub. Every time MCC's independence is mooted, someone brings up the nasty precedent of the Cricket Club of India and the Brabourne Stadium, described by Keith Miller as 'the most complete ground in the world; a cricket paradise . . . Players can live on it during the match. At night a complete dance floor is carried out and put down over the playing arena. There under the soft Indian night with millions of stars twinkling overhead, you can waltz to the strains of a carefully concealed orchestra. When you feel the need for refreshments you walk a few yards to a perfectly equipped bar. In the morning you get out of bed and look down on the pitch where a few hours later you will be playing.'*

It was not Lord's, it was certainly not The Oval. Nor is it any longer a Test match ground, as it was from 1948 to 1973. As MCC owns Lord's, so the CCI owns the Brabourne Stadium, and this was at the root of a bitter dissatisfaction between the club and the Bombay Cricket Association. The Association saw itself at the mercy of the CCI for the distribution of profits from Test matches and other first-class games played at the Brabourne, as well as for the allocation of seats for Test matches. It was not a happy arrangement, and matters came to a head when the CCI would not acquiesce to the Bombay Association's request for sufficient seats for the Test match against Tony Lewis's England side in 1972–73. No longer prepared to go on with this continual conflict, the Association decided to terminate its dependence on the CCI and build the stadium that now stages India's Test matches in Bombay and is named after the man who initiated the breakaway, S. K. Wankhede.

The spectre presented to MCC members is that Lord's will be no more than the Brabourne Stadium if the club does not fall into line with the TCCB. In most respects, however, it now has. And even if MCC were to withdraw from the TCCB, there is no reason why Lord's should not remain a major venue. The TCCB is not in a position to build another cricket ground in central London, even if it was offered London Zoo at a knockdown price. In addition to Lord's it has the use of The Oval, where many of cricket's marketing strategies were conceived, but it is unlikely that the two Tests which London stages would produce the same

* Vasant Raiji and Anandji Dossa. *CCI & The Brabourne Stadium 1937–1987* (The Cricket Club of India, 1987)

income if both those Tests were played at The Oval. Besides, cricket cannot be sold on success alone; tradition and cricket's place in English life are part of the package, and Lord's is an essential part of England's traditions in a way the Brabourne Stadium never was in India's heritage. Sponsors know that a major match at Lord's, be it a Test, one-day international or cup final, has a magic entirely its own, and they will want their games played there. It is time MCC members tested the water. David Gower's dismissal by the England selectors was simply a flash in the pan. The real issue is the essential nature of English cricket; the soul of English cricket. MCC protected it for generations of cricketers and then left it exposed to the ways of the world. It owes it to cricket and to cricketers to take up that protection once more.

I know it won't. Overall self-interest will prevail, which is why the struggle for cricket's soul is a struggle being lost. All over the British Isles, in England, Scotland, Ireland and Wales, men and women are giving their time to keep that soul alive, teaching the rudiments of cricket to children in the hope that, as well as a love of the game, they will be imbued with something of the philosophy of the game: its unique place in the nation's life, its nobility of spirit, its code of chivalry and respect. That is why they despair when a Botham spits, a Broad stands his ground, a Gatting becomes embroiled with an umpire, or half a dozen Pakistani braves converge on another umpire like apaches in pursuit of Jane Russell. It is why they are angered every time officialdom fudges issues that call for authority and not bureaucracy. And, because they are concerned for cricket as they believe it should be played, each spring they start all over again. They do not have time for the committees that run the game at the highest level: they are too busy being cricket's unsung heroes.

Run and ruin: only a first person singular pronoun separates them. Which is not to say that men go on committees only to further their own interests or boost their egos. Committees, however, have a knack of turning the best-intentioned men into committeemen, which may be why the best committeemen, like many politicians, are not always the best-intentioned men. I do not doubt that they believe in the game. They profess their love for cricket, and they love their involvement in it. But I hope they know what they are doing.

> Yet each man kills the thing he loves,
>   By each let this be heard,
> Some do it with a bitter look,
>   Some with a flattering word.
> The coward does it with a kiss,
>   The brave man with a sword!*

* Oscar Wilde. *The Ballad of Reading Gaol*

Index